Understanding Religious Abuse and Recovery

Understanding Religious Abuse and Recovery

Discovering Essential Principles for Hope and Healing

Patrick J. Knapp

Foreword by Michael Langone

PICKWICK *Publications* · Eugene, Oregon

UNDERSTANDING RELIGIOUS ABUSE AND RECOVERY
Discovering Essential Principles for Hope and Healing

Pickwick Publications
An Imprint of Wipf and Stock Publishers
199 W. 8th Ave., Suite 3
Eugene, OR 97401

www.wipfandstock.com

PAPERBACK ISBN: 978-1-7252-8649-8
HARDCOVER ISBN: 978-1-7252-8650-4
EBOOK ISBN: 978-1-7252-8651-1

Cataloguing-in-Publication data:

Names: Knapp, Patrick J., author. | Langone, Michael, foreword.

Title: Understanding religious abuse and recovery: discovering essential principles for hope and healing / by Patrick J. Knapp; foreword by Michael Langone.

Description: Eugene, OR: Pickwick Publications, 2021 | Includes bibliographical references and indexes.

Identifiers: ISBN 978-1-7252-8649-8 (paperback) | ISBN 978-1-7252-8650-4 (hardcover) | ISBN 978-1-7252-8651-1 (ebook)

Subjects: LCSH: Psychological abuse victims—Religious life. | Psychological abuse—Religious aspects. | Recovery movement—Religious aspects.

Classification: BV4596.P87 K63 2021 (print) | BV4596.P87 (ebook)

04/19/21

To Mary Knapp, the mother who modeled tenacious learning and Heidi Knapp, beloved spouse who provided consistent necessary emotional support and encouragement.

Without our lives being explained in relation to the larger picture,
we lack the glasses to see reality adequately, correctly, and coherently.
The need for the sharper vision has been replaced by a concern
for the sharper image: How do I look, feel, and come across?

—FRANCIS SCHAEFFER, 2002, P. 23

Contents

List of Illustrations

Foreword

THIS BOOK, WHICH IS based on the author's doctoral research, is scholarly in genesis and scope, yet practical in purpose. The goal of the book is to develop a counseling approach that is rooted in a thoughtful exploration of philosophical, theological, and psychological concepts pertinent to religious abuse.

The author is transparent about the fact that he operates within a Christian worldview. His perspective, however, is not a mere "bias." He explores in depth and with respect other approaches to the issue of religious abuse. He finds value in all, and he disagrees with all. That is the mark of somebody who thinks synthetically, who tries to integrate ideas that to the casual observer may seem incompatible. When it works, which it does in this book, such an integration is creative. It is a new way of looking at what exists by bringing known things together in a new framework.

This is not a "cookbook." It is not a handbook. It is not a manual. The book is not meant for people seeking simple and straightforward answers to the multifaceted problems posed by religious abuse. This is a book for people who recognize that the religious impulse springs from the depths of one's consciousness and, therefore, that the abuse of religious feeling, faith, and seeking will not be a simple phenomenon to analyze or to heal.

Dr. Knapp reviews the history of religious abuse and recent scholarly and professional literature relevant to the topic. He then evaluates the pros and cons of the most prominent approaches to the problem of religious abuse. He applies this knowledge to the development of an innovative and integrative theory of recovery, using the SECURE acronym to summarize the principles (safe haven, emotions, cognitive focus, unconditional positive regard, relationships, and education). From these principles, he derives a practical approach to helping people recover from religious abuse.

Lastly, he ends with the scholarly humility with which he began his research. He discusses what needs to be done to advance understanding of the topic.

I am pleased that such a thoughtful book has been published. I trust that the reader will agree.

Michael Langone, PhD
Executive Director *International Cultic Studies Association*
Editor-in-Chief, *ICSA Today*

Preface

THROUGHOUT HISTORY A GREAT many people have been significantly injured by those using religious beliefs for justification. This has occurred both unintentionally and sometimes with planned deliberation. Due to felt shame and discomfort in speaking about their abuse, this sort of injury happens more than we realize. Many of us have known others and/ or perhaps we ourselves, who have experienced abusive religious leaders. Understanding this abuse and finding healing from it, can be overwhelming. In this book, I seek to provide thoughtful and emotionally connective answers to serious questions about religious abuse and recovery.

Included in this book are insights from the experience of my own bible-based religious abuse (1970–1984), my recovery, and over three decades helping others heal from their abuse. The process of writing this book was also influenced by a diverse formal education. Following my undergraduate degree in psychology, was an extensive reevaluation of my theology while finishing an elongated graduate philosophy of religion program (1988–2000), then doctoral studies and counseling internships in marriage/family counseling and addictions (2010–2013); next, a PhD (pastoral psychology, 2016–2019), concluding with a thesis on religious abuse recovery.

This book originates from that doctoral thesis and may therefore be primarily of interest to academics. But, it may also be appreciated more broadly by others seeking thoughtful answers to religious abuse and perhaps themselves in need of recovery. I provide an important historical context, taken care to define specialized terms, organize various opinions on religious abuse and defend my own evolving perspective. I've sought to present material in a clear and logical way, making it user-friendly, included a subject and scripture index and suggest improvements to the field of cultic-studies. I conclude this book with updated related resources, both to enhance further research and for ongoing religious abuse recovery for those in need.

As a result of a half-century of my involvement in this field, I conclude that to best understand abuse and healing requires increasing the bandwidth of information for clarity and enhanced integration. This larger contextual approach can sharpen concepts, reject over-simplification and treat both this topic and the people negatively affected, with deep levels of compassion and appropriate seriousness.

Many thoughtful and caring people have influenced both my thinking and emotions on this subject. My major goal in writing this book has been to not only summarize the insights that I have been graciously given over many years, but to enhance the readers understanding and appreciation of religious abuse recovery. I also hope that as you read, you will be reminded that finding both insight and deep healing is achievable and recovery is always unique to the individual. This is true of the religious content to be processed, the felt needs to be explored and determining the appropriate pace and means for healing. Finally, no matter who you are, if you're ready to go beyond often unhelpful simplistic answers and explore this topic along with the rousing journey it will inevitably provide, then I encourage you to press on . . .

Acknowledgments

THIS BOOK REQUIRED THE influence of many people, used by God to shape my thinking, emotions, research and writing. There were several at the Graduate Theological Foundation, chief of which was Dr. Ann-Marie Neale, my remarkable adviser, for her ever-positive meaningful encouragement and academic direction to shape my doctoral thesis and eventually this book. Significant too, was my patient and well-informed APA thesis editor, Sharon Hamm who kept me from an abundance of writing errors and my mother, Mary M. Knapp, who, by her example, gave me a life-long tenacious love of learning.

I have been inspired by many life-mentors and their academic pursuits: Drs. Robert McGregor Wright (theology), Alan Myatt (sociology of religion), Douglas Groothuis (philosophy), Gordon Lewis (apologetics), Sharon Hilderbrant (family-systems theory), Maria Boccia (attachment theory) and Michael Langone (cultic studies). Their academic rigor, and personal friendships over many years helped to shape both my Christian faith and this book.

The steady support of my beloved spouse, Heidi Knapp, was essential. She listened to my abundant external processing and by her insightful suggestions helped to make this project achievable. Without her strong and constant emotional encouragement, I would have likely settled on an ABD, all-but-dissertation result, and certainly would have never have completed this book.

Finally, most of all, I am thankful to God, for His systematic and timely placement of all these relational influences making this book possible. Without His loving guidance and empowerment, nothing of authentic worth would have been accomplished (Phil 2:13). Above all, He is worthy of praise (Ps 100:4–5)!

Soli Deo Gloria!

Abbreviations

AA	Alcoholics Anonymous
AACC	American Association of Christian Counselors
AFF	American Family Foundation
ASCRIBED	Acronym, identifying essential recovery needs of those religiously abused:

A	Altruism
S	Self-Differentiation
C	Cognitive Acedia
R	Relational requirement
I	Identity
B	Beliefs
E	Emotional dysregulation
D	Daily needs

CBE	Christians for Biblical Equality
CESNUR	Center for studies on New Religions
CRI	Christian Research Institute
DTL	Darkness to Light
DWP	Democratic Workers Party
EMNR	Evangelical Ministries to New Religions
EFT	Emotion Focused Therapy
GCAC	Great Commission Association of Churches
GCC	Great Commission Churches

GCI	Great Commission International
GST	General Systems Theory
ICSA	International Cultic Studies Association
ICC	International Churches of Christ
ICOC	International Churches of Christ
INFORM	Informational Network Focus on Religious Movement
NEIRR	New England Institute of Religious Research
NIP	National Institute for the Psychotherapies
NRM	New Religious Movement
PBS	Public Broadcasting Service
ROP	The Religion of Peace
SECURE	Acronym, identifying essential principles of religious abuse recovery:
S	Safe Haven
E	Emotion
C	Cognitive focus
U	Unconditional positive regard
R	Relational support system
E	Education to understand family-systems theory
TACO	Totalist Aberrant Christian Organization

Introduction

It has become increasingly challenging for clergy, counselors, educators, and other helping professionals to understand the complexities of the physical, emotional, and relational abuse taking place under the name of religious belief. At the same time, a shift in the postmodern perception of how one defines truth within a continually increasing level of cultural religious pluralism has resulted in an obscured definition of traditional cultural values (Groothuis, 2000). With the explosive amount of information available from the Internet and the desire for quick and easy answers, those with an interest in cultic studies are frequently prone to accept a simplistic, piecemeal, and often reductionist understanding of others' religious beliefs and behaviors. Therefore, when they endeavor to understand harmful religious behavior and how one might recover from its effects, they can easily feel overwhelmed. In this paper, I survey some of the inherent challenges associated with this effort to understand religious abuse: (a) diverse definitions; (b) varying philosophies and theologies; (c) unclear role of mind control; (d) complexity and variability of experiences; (e) sustaining objectivity in the abused; and (f) limitations of published integrative resources (i.e., Christian apologetics, sociology, psychology, theology, cultic studies, and philosophy).

First, terminology challenges are inherent in this study (Langone, M., & Chambers, W., 1991; Langone, M., 2015); to help counter the lack of clarity in terms, this book includes a glossary (see Appendix A). The term *cult* itself can be significantly challenging (Rosedale, Langone, Bradshaw, & Eichel, 2015). For example, *cult* easily engenders unhelpful stereotyped impressions of extreme religious groups, such as the death of 918 people on November 18, 1978, at The Peoples Temple, known as the Jonestown Massacre (Layton, 1999). I have previously suggested that "By 'cult' is meant a group that holds to beliefs or practices that clearly contradict the Bible in many of its central teachings, while promoting a sinful form of dependency on others, especially on its leader" (Knapp, P., 2000, p. 4). However, the term *cult* can too easily be used in a pejorative or dismissive way to refer to those with whom we do not agree, and it now seems more meaningful and pragmatic to use a broader and more inclusive term that is easily applicable in varying degrees to all religious environments. Therefore, I do not use *cult* in this paper except when I quote others who use the term. I use the concept of *religiously abusive environment* in place of *cult*. And instead of *cultic*, I use *spiritual abuse*. I use *religious* or *spiritual* abuse synonymously. By *religious* or *spiritual abuse*, I mean:

> actions or beliefs that damage pervert or hinder one's understanding of and relationship with God. It is fundamental to our nature that we are created in God's image and designed to get our meaning from Him.
>
> The spiritual abuser encourages one to replace God by something or someone as the source of ultimate personal fulfillment. This misrepresents what it means to be made in the image of God. It strikes at the very core of who we are. (Knapp, P., n.d., para. 1)

Such a definition immediately introduces important philosophical and theological categories. Many have suggested that, knowingly or unknowingly, consistently or inconsistently, all of us have a preconceived set of philosophical beliefs about the world in which we live (e.g., Groothuis, 2011; Sire, 1976/2009).

A second and related challenge is that these fundamental beliefs provide us with a *philosophical (and theological) reference point* by which we struggle to understand ourselves, others, and more generally, the world in which we live. This reference point is commonly referred to as a *worldview* (Groothuis, 2011; Sire, 1976/2009). In affirming this universal experience as he wrote about the important contributions of the spirituality of Viktor Frankl, author and editor Melvin Kimble (2000) stated:

> [It is] axiomatic that all people have a psychotheological worldview by which they define their life purpose and nature. This psychotheological worldview is largely a product of life experience which can be identified and most readily accessed through the individual's core beliefs and their resultant thoughts and feelings. (p. 136)

Like Kimble (2000) and Frankl (1984), many individuals believe their psychological and theological beliefs shape their life goals and their sense of self-worth. The idea of a worldview, of philosophical core beliefs providing us with such a reference point, has been assumed by many philosophers (Sire, 1976/2009). Included in the term *worldview* are significant philosophic questions, one of which involve our concept of God, or as commonly referred to in Alcoholics Anonymous (AA), one's *Higher Power* (AA, 2001). The concept of a worldview introduces the term *metaphysics,* that part of philosophy concerned with the basic causes and nature of things. Additionally, a worldview includes one's view of *prime reality,* or one's *ontology,* a branch of metaphysics concerned with the nature and relations of being (Audi, 2001, pp. 563–66).

The philosophical starting point of this paper is the prime reality of God as defined in the most well-known historic Christian creeds and statements of faith: the Apostles Creed, the Nicene Creed, the Athanasian Creed, or as most comprehensively identified in the Westminster Assembly of Divines' *Confession of Faith* (1647/1976). In the Christian tradition, the concept of the *image of God* can provide a defining anthropology for understanding human needs and desires. This concept is particularly important because human needs and desires are abundantly present in the course of recovery from any significant abuse, and certainly those labeled as religious in origin. Macaulay and Barrs (1978) have suggested a helpful definition of the concept:

> The expression *the image of God* means simply "made like God." "Let us make man in our own image, after our likeness" (Gen 1:26). To say this does not mean that man was completely like God. There were differences of course: man was a limited, physical creature, male and female, who was totally dependent on the Creator not only for the origin of his existence, but also for its continuation. Nevertheless, though unlike God in important ways, man was like God because man was a person. (pp. 13–14)

Secular concepts of religious abuse typically do not incorporate one having a well-defined view of God and the nature of humankind as ultimately necessary for comprehensive recovery. Those from a faith-based perspective, however, believe otherwise (Johnson, D. & VanVonderen, 1991).

The third challenge to our understanding of religious abuse within this study is the significant differences in how one perceives the *role of mind control,* sometimes referred to as *thought reform, coercive persuasion,* or *undue influence.* This paper provides a summary of the eight interdependent and interactive behavioral themes that define the characteristics of Robert Lifton's concept of mind control or thought reform (Lifton, 1961/1989).

Within the context of these various perspectives, the following may serve as a basic behavioral definition: "Mind control denotes a set of techniques used manipulatively to unethically influence how a person thinks, feels and acts, with the purpose of creating a detrimental dependency upon another" (Knapp, P., 2000, p. 4).

Some professionals in the field attribute nearly absolute influential power to those who exercise the techniques associated with the thought-reform theory (Hassan, 1988/2015), and others deny it altogether, suggesting that people naturally elect religious choices based on their own free volition (Barker, 1984). Still others suggest a view of mind control that rejects both extremes and instead hold a more theologically and philosophically nuanced position (Knapp, P., 2000).

A fourth challenge is that the complexity and variability of religiously abusive experience, personal family history, and individual personality make meaningful dialogue about the issue challenging. Although there are many behavioral similarities in differing religious systems, each individual's internal and external experiences may differ widely, which often makes clear communication challenging. These variations require mindful attention to the various recovery issues common to religious abuse. These issues are often rather broad and typically include many categories. There are the practical issues, psychological and emotional difficulties, cognitive inefficiencies, social/personal relationship problems, and philosophical/attitudinal issues, to name a few (Singer & Lalich, 1995). Without a sufficient interpretive approach and empathetic appreciation, one's understanding of and response to the issue of religious abuse can easily be inadequate or even inappropriately dismissive.

When professionals are contending with strongly held religious or spiritual beliefs in an individual who has experienced religious abuse, they can easily identify a fifth challenge: that of contending with the individual's extreme depth and range of emotions, which can make objectivity, while not impossible, certainly arduous at best (Langone, 1993, pp. 307–14). Many writers and researchers within this field self-report as either having themselves come from, or having had a loved one involved in, religiously abusive environments. This background commonly makes their commitment to the topic of recovery deep and personal. For instance, one of the largest and most professional organizations in the world that addresses religious abuse and recovery, the International Cultic Studies Association's (ICSA's) online autobiographical profiles clearly suggest that many, if not most, of its members self-identify as having significant personal history with religious abuse (see http://www.icsahome.com/elibrary/peopleprofiles). Because the systemic effects of one's recovery from religious abuse are commonly ongoing and variable, issues of emotional *transference*, "displacement of feeling from a prior to a current object" (Yalom, 1985, p. 201) can easily affect one's ability to think clearly and can diminish appreciation for other's perspective of their religious abuse and recovery.

Finally, a sixth challenge involves the lack of broad, integrative books, articles, or papers that reflect a theoretical understanding of the process of recovery from religiously abusive environments. One possible reason for this deficiency is that most writers and researchers in this field do not have a significant background in the realms of philosophy of religion, theology and psychosocial theory while simultaneously having a personal history of religious-abuse recovery; and the practical wisdom of many years filled with assisting others in their spiritual journeys. Again, this limitation also is clearly evidenced in the ICSA's autobiographic profiles.

For individuals to have a broad and deep educational and experiential background in any field of endeavor may hold greater hope for advancements in that field in terms of both theory and praxis. Many researchers and writers have suggested ways through which people might best understand and recover from religiously abusive environments. In the chapters that follow, I seek to support others' opportunities for growth in just such an integration on the topic of religious abuse and recovery.

In chapter 1, I provide a broad overview of the history of religious abuse and identify core characteristics of four fundamental theoretical perspectives on religious abuse and recovery: a *mind-control, victimization* approach; a *deliberative or Conversionist* conceptualization (I primarily use the term *Conversionist* throughout the remaining content); a *psychosocial, needs-based* understanding, and finally, a *dynamic-systems* approach. These four perspectives include adherents who self-identify as both religious and as primarily secular. I summarize relevant literature and clearly organize the varying opinions.

A mind-control or thought-reform perspective of religious abuse asserts that it is primarily the behavioral dynamics of another's undue influence that results in a person's involvement in such religious abuse (Hassan, 1988/2015). These advocates typically make strong appeals to Lifton's (1961/1989) or Singer and Lalich's (1995) work on thought reform. Advocates of a Conversionist conceptualization deny any mind control and typically place culpability upon the free and varied choices of individuals, attributing responsibility primarily to the autonomous decisions made by those who choose to participate in what some believe are religiously abusive environments (Barker, 1984; Rhodes, 2013). A psychosocial, needs-based understanding suggests that people join, remain in, and exit from religiously abusive environments primarily because of unmet psychological and relational needs and that, at varying levels, people are mutually culpable for their involvement (Ash, 1983). Finally, a dynamic-systems approach supports the foundational notion that no one influential sphere—psychological need, imposed influence, or deliberated individual choice—plays a necessarily determinative function; instead, a variable and interconnected dynamic system perspective is essential to understand religious abuse and recovery (Langone, 1996; Knapp, P., 2000; Lalich, 2004; Johnson, D., & VanVonderen, 1991).

In chapter 2, I provide the theological and philosophical evaluative analytics that undergird this paper. I suggest an apologetic, a method of reasoned defense, for framing this discussion around the need for a Christian worldview, highlighting the unavoidability of theological presuppositions, while acknowledging the important role of social-science evidence, placing each in perspective. I clearly identify and explain theoretical source criteria. Unless otherwise indicated, when I refer to specific biblical scriptures, I use the English Standard Version (ESV). Further, I stress the role of philosophical context or presuppositions while suggesting the need for logical coherence, comprehensive evidence, existential viability, and conceptual wholeness in theorizing about religious abuse and recovery.

Significant theoretical linkage among the four broad perspectives identified in chapter 1 (the psychosocial, needs-based understanding; a mind-control, victimization approach, a deliberative or Conversionist conceptualization, and a dynamic-systems approach) provides common ground from which to derive cooperative dialogue. Unfortunately, because of clear philosophic barriers and general differences of opinion, typically around the understanding of mind control, there is commonly a strong cacophony between the various perspectives (Passantino, B., & Passantino, G., 1994; Martin, P., 1998; Barker, 1984; Singer and Lalich, 1995). For advocates of the Conversionist viewpoint, individuals' beliefs matter and ideas have consequences; mind-control adherents believe that persons may be significantly influenced by the manipulative behavior of others; for supporters of the psychosocial needs-based perspective, all humans have common social and psychic needs that inevitably result in religious or spiritual involvement; and for the dynamic-systems approach, combined elements of influence and unique individual life factors and needs must be considered. Those with each perspective attest to significant anthropological *axioms* (propositions regarded as self-evident), that inform their understanding of religious abuse and recovery.

In chapter 3, I apply the identified apologetic criteria presented in chapter 2, examining the strengths and limitations of each of the four general perspectives of understanding and recovery from religious abuse discussed in chapter 1. I suggest that no general perspective of religious abuse and recovery provides sufficient theoretical accounting of religious abuse and recovery, but that each is helpful, given the limitations of its philosophical assumptions. I then propose that a larger contextual approach which integrates theological and philosophical constructs is needed to more adequately understand involvement in and recovery from religiously abusive environments.

In chapter 4, I explain the theological cogency of understanding principles of recovery from religious abuse and advance a new perspective, SECURE. This acronym stands for the importance of the concept and practice of (a) a *Safe Haven*, which derives from attachment theory (Bowlby, 1969, 1972, 1980, 1982; Kirkpatrick, 2005); acknowledgment of (b) the essential role and function of *Emotion*, as identified in emotion-focused therapy (EFT; Johnson, S. M., 2008); (c) the importance of remaining *Cognitively focused*, drawing from cognitive behavioral theory (Beck, 2011); (d) *Unconditional positive regard*, coming from the influence of humanistic psychology (Rogers, 1956/1980); and (e) the essential benefits in a *Relational* support system, clearly found in the twelve-step plans of recovery (Dinneen, 2013); and finally, (f) affirming the need for *Education* regarding the influences of the family-of-origin, or applied family systems theory, to a religious environment (Friedman, 1985) as a unifying and interpretive context. An overview of the SECURE perspective is available in Appendix B.

In chapter 5, I discuss additional research and investigations to benefit cultic studies, and to strengthen the SECURE approach. In this final chapter, I suggest seven areas of ongoing research and how they may occur. Appendix C includes additional recovery resources for practical use and to assist in the ongoing process of theory development in the field.

I suggest in this paper that past and current perspectives on religious abuse and recovery need to be conceptually *enlarged* and *redefined*. This need for enlarging and redefining one's concept of reality is commonly suggested in forms of existential analysis, or logotherapeutic approaches to therapy (Frankl, 1997/2011). Such an approach, which involves a systemic perspective and ideally includes philosophical, psychological, social, and theological considerations, may better account for the recovery needs of those affected by religious abuse. Finally, within this thesis, I acknowledge the value of varying viewpoints about how people recover from religious abuse and suggest the need for those with an interest in cultic studies to sharpen their conceptual understanding of recovery with the intent of encouraging increased collaboration and better practice. My intent is to explore and integrate features from various conceptual frameworks, to identify the main sources of recovery from religious abuse, and to present a cohesive and comprehensive perspective based on the principles typically identified in family systems (Walsh, 2003) and attachment theory (Bowlby, 1969, 1972, 1980, 1982), with an implicit view of truth that originates from a Christian worldview (Groothuis, 2000).

1

Historical Overview

RELIGIOUS ABUSE HAS A broad, significant, and painful worldwide history (Cowan & Bromley, 2008; Engh, 2007; Singer & Lalich, 1995; Stark & Corcoran, 2014). Some professionals in the field have chosen to write about religious abuse specifically within the context of the Christian church (Frend, 1981; Foxe & Wright, 1811); others have focused deeply within the history of particular groups (Giambalvo & Rosedale, 1996; Lindsey, 2014; Tanner & Tanner, 1989). In the first section of this chapter, I highlight the historical relevance of abuse under religiously motivated behaviors and belief. This discussion is not intended to be comprehensive; instead it will address only some of the more significant representative occurrences of religious abuse while placing them in a historical and relevant cultural context.

The second and larger section of this chapter includes a general review of relevant literature in the field of religious abuse and recovery as expressed from four basic theoretical perspectives on religious abuse and recovery: a mind-control, victimization approach; a psychosocial, needs-based understanding; a deliberative or Conversionist conceptualization; and finally, a dynamic-systems approach. These perspectives include adherents who self-identify as faith based and others who appeal to a secular orientation. I distinguish varying opinions, and identify both organized and assorted contributions to this field of study.

Section 1: Historical Relevance of the Problem

Depending on one's primary intent, each of several approaches to reviewing the history and relevance of spiritual abuse over time might be appealing, and choosing among them can be difficult. For instance, some researchers may wish to begin their historical focus on recent occurrences of blatant religious abuse to make the subject more manageable. For them, the Jonestown Massacre (1978) provides just such an example. Starting at this historic juncture is tempting; it significantly shortens the historical narrative of religious abuse and is an easily identifiable target because of the 913 members who lost their lives in Guyana, South America (Layton, 1999). Similarly, on our own shores, one might suggest the history behind the infamous 1993 Waco Massacre as a starting place (Thibodeau & Whiteson, 1999).

Others who hold a Christian theological persuasion might suggest looking to some of the earliest written records, citing the account of the Garden of Eden (Gen 3) and what is commonly referred to as the Fall of humankind as indicative of the source and earliest identifiable cause of religious or spiritual abuse (Wright, K., 2001, p. 90–91). This choice too is tempting because it suggests a theological context from which to better understand religious abuse and recovery that includes important presuppositional philosophical constructs. These worldview assumptions include the nature of humankind, the source of the human dilemma, and ultimately a redemptive or restorative solution (Schaeffer, 1968).

Still others have focused on more recent times and more broadly sociological factors, identifying religious abuse across all belief systems (Stark & Corcoran, 2014). A benefit of this approach is that it acknowledges the universality of various religious abuses commonly identified both in recent history and throughout all religious persuasions.

Combining the strengths of each of these approaches, however, potentially provides a more comprehensive, anthropological context and therefore a theoretical benefit to both this chapter and this thesis as a whole. Accordingly, I have chosen to begin with the second option, citing the Garden of Eden (Gen 3) as the source and earliest identifiable cause of religious or spiritual abuse; proceed through the significant and well-known occurrences represented in the first suggestion, focusing on the recent historical accounts of blatant religious abuse; and finally conclude with the universal sociological characteristics noted in the third approach that identify religious abuse across belief systems.

I begin with the Bible's account of the Garden of Eden as the historical source of religious abuse and a starting point for understanding recovery because it has already been suggested that, ~~knowingly or unknowingly, consistently or inconsistently, individuals start their evaluations of self and others through a worldview that requires a philosophical or theological interpretative understanding of reality.~~ If one holds to a high view of biblical inspiration and authority, as suggested in the next chapter, then it stands to reason that the historical account of moral failure presented in Genesis 3 as the first recorded occasion of religious abuse may provide a helpful context for understanding the religious abuse that has followed since. It might also provide some helpful indicators of how recovery from religious abuse may occur. Assuming this as our starting place, what does the Bible say about this topic? Consider the following comments from one researcher, Gary R. Veenhuizen (2011), in his doctoral dissertation:

> The term "spiritual abuse" was coined about thirty years ago in the book, *The Subtle Power of Spiritual Abuse,* by D. Johnson and VanVonderen (1991). However, the issue has been with us since Satan questioned the words of God in the Garden of Eden (Gen 3 KJV), to further his own sedition. Hoping to influence and corrupt this new creation, he re-interpreted God's directive, distorting and misrepresenting the order, resulting in an egocentric conclusion that plunged humanity into a cycle of sin and abuse.
>
> The word sin in the OT [Old Testament], *chata'* (חָטָא), refers to one's personal offense, to lead astray or to the harm he has done (Bauer, Arndt, & Gingrich, 1957, p. 38). This would include relational offenses to another that rise to this definitional level. Sin is the root and result of abuse because it distorts and defiles the human creation made in the "image of God" (Gen 1:27). We say the root because sin, the ultimate self-indulgence, is the impetus that causes people to abuse others and the result because sin is the outcome. (pp. 40–41)

As Veenhuizen (2011) suggested, this reference point can provide a theological starting place for a historical understanding of religious abuse. In addition to the use of the Garden of Eden as the initial reference point, the writings of the Old Testament prophetic books provide many examples and denunciations of spiritual abuse (Ezek 34:1–24; Jer 5:26–31; Zech 11). Each of these representative passages conveys the common denominators of religiously abusive leaders being guilty of evil deeds, failure to defend those under their care, neglect, falsity, self-centeredness, and injustice, all of which result in condemnation by the God of scripture. One section of the Ezekiel passage is illustrative:

> The word of the Lord came to me: "Son of man, prophesy against the shepherds of Israel; prophesy and say to them: 'This is what the Sovereign Lord says: Woe to you shepherds of Israel who only *take care of yourselves!* Should not shepherds take care of the flock? You eat the curds, clothe yourselves with the wool and slaughter the choice animals, but you *do not take care of the flock.* You have *not strengthened the weak or healed the sick or bound up the injured.* You have not *brought back the strays or searched for the lost.* You have *ruled them harshly and brutally.* So they were scattered because there was no shepherd, and when they were scattered they became food for all the wild animals. My sheep wandered over all the mountains and on every high hill. They were scattered over the whole earth, and *no one searched or looked for them.*'" (Ezek 34:1–6 NIV; emphasis added)

In addition to the Old Testament providing many clear historical descriptions of and exhortations against religious abuse, there also are many New Testament examples. Thematic examples in each of the four Gospels, with corrective statements attributed to Jesus, include Matthew 9:35–38; Mark 6:33–34; Luke 15:1–2; and John 10:11–13. In each of these, as in the Old Testament scriptures, religiously motivated abusive behaviors and values are described. It also has been suggested that

> The Gospels present numerous pictures of ways people are hurt by abusive spiritual systems in another way: by legalistic attack. It takes only a superficial reading of the New Testament to see that Jesus was not at odds with "sinners"—the prostitutes, lepers and the demonized–but with the religious system of that day. (Johnson, D., & VanVonderen, 1991, p. 31)

These writers, D. Johnson (pastor) and VanVonderen (addictions interventionist and professor; 1991), additionally state,

> Little wonder that it was part of Jesus' mission to expose an abusive system. It's important to remember four things about His confrontations. First, His confrontations landed on those who saw themselves as God's official spokespersons—the most religious, the best performers. They gave money, attended church and had more Scripture memorized than anyone. They set the standard for everyone else. Second, Jesus broke the religious rules by confronting those in authority out loud. Third, He was

treated as the problem because He said there was a problem. And fourth, crowds of broken people rushed to Him because His message offered hope and rest (p. 36).

In *The Subtle Power of Spiritual Abuse*, Johnson D. and VanVonderen (1991) have provided a plethora of examples of religious abuse outside of the four Gospels during the time the New Testament was written, and they suggest many helpful correctives. One such corrective follows, as illustrative of the imposed mind control that abusive groups used for those in Rome during the time of that writing and certainly found in our present day:

> In Romans 12:2, Paul says, "Do not be conformed to this world, but be transformed by the renewing of your mind." Don't be conformed but be transformed. Now the word *conformed* means "squeezed from the outside in." So Paul is saying, "Don't be squeezed." In a performance-focused church or family, that verse might be applied like this, "Our church or leader is right; we have a truer, purer 'word' from God than others. Therefore, we must adhere to our formula or brand of Christianity as hard and fast as possible—so we won't become like those out there who don't think as we do. If I do not live up to all I've been taught here, I will be letting God down." This orientation squeezes people from the outside in. They are not transformed, they are conformed. Transformation is an inside-out job; not outside-in. Don't allow yourself to be squeezed. Be transformed! (pp. 66–67)

This sort of imposed religiosity was common in many segments of Christendom in the first century following the death of Jesus Christ. Examples are easily identifiable in the Apostle Paul's letter to believers in the Roman province of Galatia (modern-day Turkey), in which Paul wrote, "For freedom Christ has set us free; stand firm therefore, and do not submit again to a yoke of slavery" (Gal 5:1), and he reiterates this guidance to another group of Christians from the ancient town of Corinth: "You were bought with a price; do not become bondservants of men" (1 Cor 7:23). As a summary regarding the Bible and religious abuse, consider how it is that the terms *spiritual abuse* or *religious abuse* are not explicitly defined in either the Old Testament or the New Testament, but the concept is abundant in examples throughout scripture. The Old Testament prophets, the New Testament writers, and Jesus Christ himself all made a concerted effort to identify and counter the presence of religiously abusive behavior in their culture and time. To deny this plethora of information and the importance of recovery from spiritual or religious abuse, and not to develop a clear understanding of its place in human experience, could essentially be seen as a denial of the reality of the Christian faith itself.

Thankfully, both the evidence of religious abuse and necessary correctives are easily identifiable in both the Old and New Testaments. But such abuse nevertheless continues to be experienced in many present-day Christian organizations (Clark, D., 1998) and in other religious belief systems (Martin, W., & Zacharias, 2003). But lest I jump too quickly, consider what might be identified as a historic trail that leads to current examples of religious abuse.

How might one begin to get one's arms around the past two thousand years of religious history? At the same time, how can one do this without feeling overwhelmed? One way may be to view history within a tightly contained and highlighted overview of eight historical segments of time. Within each of these segments are pivotal representative examples of blatant, religiously abusive behaviors that may help professionals in the field to understand the systemic and pervasive nature of religious abuse throughout history:

- Early Church History (Pentecost–AD 300): Jewish and Christian persecution
- The Roman Empire (AD 300–590): Persecution—both received and carried out
- The Middle Ages (AD 590–517): Rise of the papacy and related abuse
- The Reformation (AD 1517–1648): Protestant formation and reactionary abuses
- The Enlightenment (AD 1648–1789): Humanist reactions and counter-reactions
- The Nineteenth Century: Papal infallibility, revivals, and revolutions
- The Twentieth Century: Jonestown; Waco
- The Twenty-First Century–9/11: Israeli/Arab conflict and the rise of atheism

Early Church History (Pentecost–AD 300)

The highly respected first-century Jewish historian Flavius Josephus (c. AD 37–100) was simultaneously a religious Pharisee, soldier, informant to the

Romans, and historical writer. Translated from the original Greek, his most extensive writings on ancient Jewish history are still in existence. Many scholars suggest that the compilation of Josephus's writings (AD 97) represents an invaluable collection of writing for those wanting to study ancient history (Josephus & Whiston, 2003). Included in these combined works is an autobiographical account of Josephus's own life (pp. 1–29); *The Antiquities of the Jews* (pp. 30–650), a historical account of the Jewish people, with the first half following the Hebrew Scriptures and the second half containing an active participant account of the Jewish people beyond the biblical text to the time of the Jewish war against Rome (AD 66–73); *The War of the Jews* (pp. 651–925), containing Josephus's account of the preceding events and culminating with the destruction of Jerusalem, and specifically the second Jewish temple (AD 70) and the immediate aftermath; and finally, *Flavius Josephus Against Apion* (pp. 926–73), which contains Josephus's defense of the Jews against the anti-Jewish teachings of an Alexandrian schoolmaster. During the course of these writings, Josephus quoted other ancient historians (most of whose works have been lost). Throughout his writings he has shared with his readers many apolitical accounts of religiously abusive behaviors indicative of the culture and the times.

Present day theologians, commenting on the first-century can provide some helpful cultural critique regarding religious abuse of the time:

> Rome was cruel, and its cruelty can perhaps be best pictured by the events which took place in the arena in Rome itself. People seated above the arena floor watched gladiator contests and Christians thrown to the beasts. Let us not forget why the Christians were killed. They were not killed because they worshiped Jesus. . . . Nobody cared who worshiped whom so long as the worshiper did not disrupt the unit of the state, *centered in the formal worship of Caesar.* (Schaeffer, 1976, p. 24; emphasis added)

Religiously motivated beliefs resulted in extreme behavioral abuse. This approach of intertwining religion and politics has been prevalent throughout history, and commonly, under the justification of religious belief, the results are unavoidable abuse.

The Roman Empire (AD 300–590)

Two impactful events drove this segment of time and highlight the continued religious abuse of the day. First was perhaps the most violent and systematic persecution ever imposed upon Christians—imprisonment, death, and all sorts of torture and cruelty, perpetrated by the reigning emperors Diocletian (284–305) and Galerius (305–11) because of the politics of the day, couched in the Christians' refusal to perform sacrifices to the Roman gods (Frend, 1986, p. 319).

Second, following a dream and a related military victory (312), then-emperor Constantine became very supportive of the Christian church. He issued the Edict of Milan (January 313), proclaiming the free exercise of religion and the reimbursement from his own treasury of those who had suffered loss during the earlier persecution. The negative result of this edict, however, was that the spheres of earthly government and spiritual care quickly became heavily enmeshed, and the Christian church at the end of the century became not only the established religion of the empire, but also prone to abusive political authority. With these changes came the secularization of the church, and this reversal meant the punishment of non-Christians, which culminated in emperor Theodosius (380) determining that Christian belief was a matter of imperial command rather than personal choice upon reflection. Theodosius's will and his perception of God's will become virtually identical and resulted in the emperor's command to his armies to kill seven thousand Thessalonians in punishment for their resistance to what he perceived as his demagogic status. Although Theodosius did eventually publicly repent, as required by Ambrose, the well-respected Catholic bishop of Milan, under threat of excommunication, rarely did a bishop ever step so far into the political fray again (Shelley, 1995, pp. 96–97). The description of this political/religious environment leads naturally to the next segment of history to consider.

The Middle Ages (AD 590–517)

This period commonly has been referred to as the Dark Ages because it was, in many respects, a time of chaos and disarray. Significant political, religious, and social changes were taking place, most of them easily attributable to momentous religious events. A brief overview of this historic period is replete with examples of religiously motivated behavior, much of which was clearly abusive and deadly (Armstrong, 2014/2015).

The Crusades (1096–1291), it has been said, were a series of religious and political wars, which some historians have proposed were initiated by Pope Urban II for the control of the Holy Land, while others have contended that Islamic aggression fueled the fires of war. There is considerable dispute about the precipitating causes of these religious wars (Maalouf & Rothschild, 2012; Runciman, 2001), but it is common knowledge that the extreme bloodshed in both Christian and Muslim ventures, while political, was also significantly motivated by religiously driven agendas; and that legacy continues to this day. In a seminal work on the crusades, Thomas Asbridge (2010) concluded:

> Perhaps the crusades do have things to tell us about our world. Most, if not all, of their lessons are common to other eras of human history. These wars lay bare the power of faith and ideology to inspire fervent mass movements and to elicit violent discord; they affirm the capacity of commercial interests to transcend the barriers of conflict; and they illustrate how readily suspicion and hatred of the "other" can be harnessed. But the notion that the struggle for dominion of the Holy Land—waged by Latin Christians and Levantine Muslims so many centuries ago—does, or somehow should, have a direct bearing upon the modern world is misguided. The reality of these medieval wars must be explored and understood if the forces of propaganda are to be assuaged, the incitements to hostility countered. But the crusades must *also* be placed where they belong: in the past. (p. 681; emphasis added)

Religiously motivated behavior that results in pain, suffering, and death is exemplified in this segment of history, and the ripples are still evident in our own time. Indeed, the past bloody Islamic history is vital to understanding the ongoing motivation (Jihad) for the political and religious tension in the Arab/Israeli conflict (Al Fadi, n.d.). No period in history and no religious group remain innocent in the course of bloody and abusive religious behaviors (Armstrong, 2014/2015).

Another particularly illustrative manifestation of religious abuse occurred during this period in what has been referred to as the Catholic Inquisition (1231–1531). It began with Pope Innocent III deciding in 1208 that the most urgent threat to the Catholic hold upon the people was that of heresy; instigating what we know today as a series of Catholic Inquisitions (Engh, 2007). This period included some of the most egregious, religiously motivated abuses ever propagated by the Catholic Church. Beginning in France, and spreading to Spain and Portugal, the Catholic Church appointed inquisitors who researched the reasons behind various difficult-to-manage regions. These inquisitors questioned people intensively about their beliefs, initially beginning with those of recent conversion from Jewish and Muslim background, but eventually including all people within their reach.

These inquisitors were supposed to identify what was deemed heretical and served as judges, with the resulting punishment typically turned over to civil officials. All levels of torture, including burning at the stake, confiscation of property, and virtually anything else the inquisitors deemed commensurate with the persons' errant beliefs and behaviors took place under the guise of religiously motivated actions. People were strongly encouraged, and sometimes tortured, to give up children, parents, and other individuals to the hands of these inquisitors. Consider too just a few of the documented statements attributed to Pope Innocent III and what the words might suggest: "The Pope is the meeting point between God and man . . . who can judge all things and be judged by no one" (Sermon 2, *Patrologia Latina 217*, p. 658); "Every cleric must obey the pope, even if he commands what is evil; for no one may judge the pope" (Consecration Sermon, c. 1200); and "Anyone who attempts to construe a personal view of God which conflicts with Church dogma must be burned without pity" (papal bull, AD 1198).

Indeed, many believers were burned alive; most famous of these were Joan of Arc (1431) and John Hus (1415). Some historians have suggested that the reaction to these abuses found in the various Catholic Inquisitions resulted in the next segment of religious abusive history, the Protestant Reformation (Armstrong, 2015, pp. 242–44).

The Protestant Reformation (1517–1648)

Protestant theologian and church historian Philip Schaff (1819–1893) wrote an eight-volume work, *History of the Christian Church* (1876), in which he stated,

> The Reformation of the sixteenth century is, next to the introduction of Christianity, the greatest event in history. It marks the end of the Middle Ages and the beginning of modern times. Starting from religion, it gave, directly or indirectly, a mighty impulse to every forward movement, and made Protestantism the chief propelling force in the history of modern civilization. (chapter 1, para. 1.)

Indeed, the Protestant Reformation was an important segment of our history. The beginning of this period, seen by some as a schism of the Catholic Church, is identified by the nailing of the 95 theses on a church door in

Wittenberg Germany (October 31, 1517) by Augustinian monk Martin Luther (1483–1546), frequently identified as founding father of the Reformation. Luther, who some have suggested has had more written about him than any other person who ever lived except for Jesus Christ (Kurian & Smith, 2010, p. 439), was soundly persecuted, along with others of his followers, for their objections to what the writers have viewed as abuses in Catholic beliefs and behaviors (Shelley, 1995).

But many good and sufficient reasons have been presented in support of the need to reform the church of the day (MacCulloch, 2015). In addition to the very negatively viewed Catholic practice of the selling Indulgences, some of the most commonly identified reasons are reflected in five positive theological affirmations (Stetzer, 2017) that were denied core teachings of the Catholic Church:

- *Sola Scriptura*: The Scripture alone is the Christian standard; the Bible alone is the ultimate authority, not the traditions or writings of the church;

- *Soli Deo Gloria*: For the glory of God alone is to be one's motivation, and all human activity is sacred, not the monastic division of life into sacred and secular perpetuated by the church;

- *Solo Christo*: It is by the work of Christ, as the sole mediator between God and man, that salvation occurs, not through the veneration of religious relics or persons;

- *Sola Gratia*: Salvation is by grace alone, not by works of penitence or self-merit; faith is imputed, not earned; and

- *Sola Fide*: Justification comes by faith alone, individually and actively trusting the merits and sacrifice of Christ to live life, not mere intellectual assent to a creed.

Some theologians have suggested that having a theological understanding and appreciation housed in these foundational Reformation principles is essential to an understanding of and recovery from religious abuse (Martin, W., & Zacharias, 2003; Rhodes, 2013). Whether this is true or not, one can easily and rightfully cite spiritual or religious abuse-motivated behaviors on the Protestant side of the Reformation.

Such abuse can be illustrated in the silence and tacit approval of Genevan French Reformer John Calvin (1509–1564) of the burning of Spanish physician Michael Servetus (1553), who was fleeing Catholic persecution for his heresy in denying the doctrine of the Trinity as he sought refuge in Geneva. In Calvin's silence and various statements, he virtually condemned Michael Servetus, earning for himself the acclaimed notoriety of being "the man who burned Servetus" (Shelley, 1995, p. 260). Like Calvin, Luther directly supported extreme abuse under the guise of religious belief in the burning of those persons deemed to be witches (Johnson, P., 1976, pp. 309–10). In this action, both Calvin and Luther appealed to a common Protestant reference to Scripture, "Thou shalt not suffer a witch to live" (Exod 22:18).

Returning to Martin Luther, one finds his legacy of anti-Semitism (Gritsch, 2012). This fact is remarkable and quickly deflates any notion that he, at least in his attitudes, was any different from many other religious leaders of his day. Thankfully, this viewpoint was not uniform among all the Reformers (Ross, 2010). And lest one become overly critical of the Catholic Church before the Reformation, it is important to remember the informed observations by Protestant, historian, and distinguished Sociology of Religion professor at Baylor University, Rodney Stark: "The rise of Protestantism was anything but the triumph of tolerance: it was a criminal offense to say Mass in Lutheran Germany; John Calvin tolerated no dissenters; and Henry VIII *burned* dissenters" (Stark, 2014, p. 263).

Culpability abounds on all sides of those participating in the Reformation. Resulting guilt for abuse under the justification of religiously motivated belief was widespread, and I explore this universal theme further shortly.

Meanwhile, following immediately on the heels of the Reformation was the now well-respected Pilgrim, John Bunyan, who was unjustly imprisoned from 1660 to 1672, and again in the winter and spring of 1675 and 1676, for preaching that was contrary to the powerful and abusive Anglican state church of his day (Bunyan, Beaumont, & Furlong, 1978). During this period, Bunyan wrote the well-known and highly acclaimed *Pilgrim's Progress* (1675) while experiencing severe physical, emotional, and relational deprivation living separated from his wife and four children, one of whom was blind. In this metaphorical narrative, he highlights the inherent challenges of Christian growth and development. The writing of *Pilgrim's Progress* (1675) was directly shaped by Bunyan's religious beliefs that were contrary to the prevailing beliefs of those in religious/political control in England (Ford, C., & Bunyan, J., 2016). The prevalence of religious abuses during this period suggests a reaction that some historians speculate supported the rise of humanistic secularism during the Enlightenment, theperiod of history that followed (Johnson, P., 1976).

The Enlightenment (AD 1648–1789)

Following the earlier eras of extreme religious turmoil and related abuses came a period during which exploring human ideals took precedence over basing one's worldview on the controlling views of religious and civil institutions. Clear, unambiguous, secular-humanist values took priority over dogma, blind faith, and superstition in the areas of tolerance, religious liberty, government, education, reason, logic, criticism, and freedom of thought. Recent advances and scientific discovery in physics, mathematics, astronomy, and biology supported this change in focus. Another key development during this period was that of a strongly supported Deism, the belief that God allows the universe to operate according to natural law, with no supernatural interference, and this evolution brought a resurgence of skepticism about things religious (Brown, 1990, pp. 197–214).

In turn, one cultural response to the movement toward secular humanism was a resurgence of Reformation thought evident in the Protestant religious revival now known as the *First Great Awakening* (1730–1745), which respected historian and author Paul Johnson (1997), referred to as "the proto-revolutionary event, the formative moment" (p. 116) that made the American Revolutionary War (1775–1783) and "could not have taken place without this religious background" (p. 117). Religious movements have indeed incredibly shaped our political and cultural history, sometimes to our good, sometimes to our detriment when they result in religious abuses.

One key figure of the First Great Awakening (1730–1745) was Jonathan Edwards (1703–1758). Edwards wrote extensively about the religious excesses and abuses prevalent in his day (Edwards, Ramsey, Smith, & Goen, 2009). His various writings culminated in a classic Reformed literary work of religious history and commentary, *Treatise Concerning the Religious Affections* (1746). In this work, Edwards thoughtfully provided readers, both then and now, with distinguishing marks of healthy and unhealthy forms of Christianity in both internal reflection and external expression. Like John Bunyan before, Edwards was an influential Protestant pastor, and he strove to provide positive correctives to the various damaging religious beliefs and behaviors of his day (Edwards & Houston, 1996). This popular work notwithstanding, the latter half of the eighteenth century saw a rejection by many of regular church services as people broadly came to believe that God did not play an important role in normal, everyday life. Part of the consequence of this change was that the following century fared no better in its encounter with religious challenges and misadventures (Singer & Lalich, 1995).

The Nineteenth Century

Some professionals in the field have reflected on the link between current religiously abusive groups and those of the nineteenth century. Clinical psychologist and emeritus adjunct professor at the University of California, Berkeley, Margaret Singer, and author, sociology professor, former cult member, and cult-information specialist, Janja Lalich, suggested that the presence of contemporary cults are rooted in the religious turmoil represented in the socioeconomic shifts that occurred during the early to mid-nineteenth century (Singer & Lalich, 1995, p. 31). Well-known sociology of religion authors (Bromley & Hammond, 1987), likewise, attribute the rapid social and economic shifts in US society as significant factors in the development of various sects or new religious movements seeking to fill the existential felt needs within the United States.

During the nineteenth century, one of the most dominant historical figures, Charles Grandison Finney (1792–1875), is broadly thought to have significantly contributed to the religious climate of the day (Noll, 1992). Finney was a leading theologian and Protestant pastor. Historian and professor Mark Noll (1992) of the University of Notre Dame, who specializes in the history of Christianity within the United States, wrote:

> A good case can be made that Finney should be ranked with Andrew Jackson, Abraham Lincoln, and Andrew Carnegie . . . as one of the most important public figures in nineteenth-century America. Beyond doubt, he stands by himself as the crucial figure in white American evangelicalism after Jonathan Edwards. (p. 176)

What did Finney contribute to our topic? Some have suggested that, more than any of his contemporaries, he contributed much to the general influence of religious abuse, not only in his day, but ultimately to ours, as well (Speed, 2015). To this point, pastor and author William P. Farley (2006) has suggested that Finney was abusively influential: He undervalued historical theology and church history, which led to his being uneducable and incorrigible; believed he was the first one to authentically understand religious revival, this despite the previous First Great Awakening (1730–1745) and his denial of very significant historical Christian doctrines, large portions of the Westminster Confession, that he had sworn to uphold and then lied about.

Similar criticism of Finney came from historian Nathan Hatch (1989): "Finney began his own religious quest, by denying the force of inherited religious authority. He relied upon his own enlightened, albeit theologically untutored, reason" (p. 199). This posture excluded Finney from historical confessional Christianity on many significant doctrinal issues. Some of these we have already noted. Farley (2006) continued,

> His second weakness, which is related to the first, was the eleva-tion of reason over revelation. Finney demanded that many bib-lical mysteries be pressed into rational human formulas. Finney struggled to "adjust the truths of Christianity into such a harmo-nious system of thought that no violence should be done to the dictates of reason," observes Murray. "This, as he often said, was (after that of the actual conversion of souls) the great aim of his life"(Murray, 1994, p. 256). Finney could not accept mysteries, like the congruence of the sovereignty of God and the responsibility of man.

Charles Finney, through his errant theology, his manipulative prac-tice, and widespread influence, contributed significantly to the religious abuses of his day that have lingered on in today's religious scene in the form of semi-Pelagianism (Challies, 2014). Both today's Catholic (Ziegler, 2014) and also most Protestant authorities (Erickson, 1998, pp. 651, 629, 649–50; Wright, R. K. M., 1996, pp. 20, 21, 53, 70) affirm the severe dangers of Pelagianism as significantly heretical throughout many church councils and therefore easily supportive of religiously abusive behaviors (Slick, n.d.). Leaving the nineteenth century behind and shifting to the more contem-porary scene, one is quickly reminded of two pivotal events in the 20th century that are representative examples of religious abuse.

The Twentieth Century

For many people who lived through the 1950s and 1960s, there is hardly a more graphic accounting of religious abuse than the survivors' stories in the first published account by staff correspondents of the *San Francisco Chronicle* (Kilduff & Javers, 1978) following the murder-suicide of 912 people, 267 of whom were children, on November 18, 1978, in Jonestown, Guyana (Layton, 1999), or the death or severe emotional/psychological injury of those at the Branch Davidian compound in Waco, Texas that culminated April 19, 1993, after a 51-day siege imposed by the federal government (Samples, 1994). Both events provide valuable insights to understanding religious abuse.

In the first event, the feature-length documentary/drama *Jonestown: Paradise Lost* (Sherman & Wolochatiuk, 2006) chronicles the Jonestown story as told by those who were deeply involved and damaged, is insightful. Easily identifiable within this story are all the telltale signs of totalitarian abuse found in unhealthy religious environments. These include illicit control of money, illicit relationships, abusive sexual behavior, political manipulation, drugs, guns, severe physical and emotional beatings, and all the behavioral characteristics consistent with brainwashing or mind control Robert Jay Lifton (1961/1989) identified in his classic work, *Thought Reform and the Psychology of Totalism*. I discuss the description and application of Lifton's work to religious abuse in the second portion of this chapter. Sadly, many have all but forgotten this tragic part of religious history, and those who have some knowledge often reduce it to a remote occurrence of religion gone badly.

Similar to, yet different from, the extreme examples of religious abuse and devastation of Jonestown is the second, more recent and geographically closer event that resulted in a disastrous end in 1993 on the final day at Mount Carmel Center and the Branch Davidian compound in Waco, Texas (Doyle, Wessinger, & Wittmer, 2012). This accounting of religious abuse, combined with what some suggest as an uninformed and misguided governmental response, led to an easily identifiable and predictive outcome on our own shores (Breault & King, 1993). Similar to Jonestown, the related events of Waco have been written about by many, from varying perspectives: former members' still loyal to the Branch Davidian group, and specifically it's deceased leader (Doyle et al., 2012; Thibodeau & Whiteson, 1999); disaffected former members, with more mixed reviews (Breault & King, 1993); the news media, with various perspectives (Reavis, 1995); many sociologists (Bromley & Melton, 2002 (pp. 149–68); theologians and Christian apologists (CRI, 2009; Newport, K., 2006; Samples, 1994); psychologist, (Singer & Lalich, 1995); governmental agencies (Dennis, 1993); and others who, had they lived during the fall the final days of the Branch Davidian compound, would have written with considerable input and passion (Martin, W., 1980).

Many of the facts surrounding the events that led up to and culminated in the destruction of the Branch Davidian compound are much in dispute (Doyle, Wessinger, & Wittmer, 2012; Thibodeau, 1999). However, as with all unhealthy religious systems, certain classic behavioral features found within the Branch Davidians were readily identifiable even before the culmination of events with the Waco fire:

- Extreme child abuse (e.g., physical beatings until the child was bruised and bleeding, and isolation);

- Beatings of disobedient members;

- Severe food deprivation as punishment;

- Outside family ties severed;

- Sleep deprivation of members; (Marc Breault, as cited in CRI, 2009, footnotes 43–47)

- The use of fear and intimidation against members who disagreed with Koresh; and

- Isolation from ex-members (David Bunds, as cited in CRI, 2009, footnotes 48–49).

Others have highlighted these typical characteristics and more as indicative of a toxic sort of faith (Arterburn & Felton, 1991). Such so-called faith occurs in diverse forms, and in both Christian practices (Orlowski, 2010) and virtually any other religious systems (Hexham & Poewe, 2000).

The Twenty-First Century

Most people today are well aware of what seems like another religiously motivated wake-up call in the destruction of the Twin Towers, World Trade Center (September 11, 2001), commonly referred to as 9/11. This event resulted in the death of at least 2,700 men, women, and children and the injury of more than 6,000 others. There are many other accounts of radical Islamic terrorism, driven by the religious belief of the necessity of Jihad, suggested by some as a radicalized form of the Muslim faith (Stark & Corcoran, 2014, pp. 77–89). Others have suggested that this singular occurrence pales in light of incidents of Islamic terrorism in 2016, with more than 1,200 occasions of such terrorism in 50 countries that have resulted in more than 11,000 people killed and more than 14,000 injured (TROP, n.d.).

Although different interpretations of these events and their related facts may have detractors based on the facts presented, the events provide a cumulative and vivid illustration that religious belief often results in severe personal abuse and death. We live today in a time when abuse by those professing strong, faith-based beliefs is pervasive and abundantly clear (Stark & Corcoran, 2014). And even those abusive individuals and groups strongly opposed to any theistic endorsement bring focus as well to the religious abuses.

In reaction to various religious abuses, a significant and growing movement of atheism is taking center stage today like never before, as documented by the Public Religion Research Institute (PRRI; Cooper, Cox, Lienesch, & Jones, 2016). Such sociological research of modern-day culture often cites the significant increase in atheistic literature as a response to the religious abuse of our day. Stark and Corcoran (2014) stated, "In the past several years an explosion of popular books by angry and remarkably nasty atheists have hit the bestseller list" (p. 65):

- *The God Delusion* by Richard Dawkins (2006)

- *Breaking the Spell* by Daniel C. Dennett (2006)

- *God is Not Great: How Religion Poisons Everything* by Christopher Hitchens (2007)

Counter to atheism as being somehow a helpful corrective, sociologists such as Rodney Stark and Katie Corcoran (2014) compare the notion of atheism being an answer to religious woes by wholly liberating oneself from religion to that of eliminating academic failure by doing away with education (pp. 123–30). But certainly, there are some who would disagree.

In *Losing My Religion* (2009), William Lobdell, articulate investigative journalist with the *Los Angeles Times* and now professor at the University of California, offers readers a personal account of his own loss of faith through his various observations of religious abuse. He reflects on articulate and implied questions that are present in the minds of both believers and nonbelievers. Lobdell (2009) does a service in identifying these concerns and experiences: As he points out in chapter 10, *Millstones Around Their Necks*, Jesus had plenty to say about the religious abuse of others (pp. 135–49). In his statement, he perhaps unknowingly supports the proposition, as previously suggested, that the Bible provides legitimate hope that religious abuse will be brought to light (2 Tim 3:1–9), and that restoration from the hands of religious abusers and charlatans is not only possible, but assured (1 Tim 4:1–16).

In support of Lobdell's (2009) objections to blatant religious abuse, one can easily identify a plethora of recently published personal accounts of contemporary religious abuse, dissatisfaction, and disillusionment along with a host of important lessons learned (e.g., Doyle et al., 2012; Hassan, 2015; Lindsey, 2014; Thibodeau & Whiteson, 1999). Recently retired Westmont College sociologist Dr. Ron Enroth (1940) made it his passionate life's work to identify recent various examples of religious abuse, and he has suggested what recovery might entail (Enroth, 1992, 1994). Many other sociologists have chronicled the universal presence of religious abuse (Conway & Siegelman, 1995; Galanter, 1989; Hargrove, 1989; Robbins & Anthony, 1990; Stark & Bainbridge, 1985).

Prolific authors Dr. Rodney Stark and Dr. Katie Corcoran, from the Institute for Studies of Religion at Baylor University, remind readers of the broad scope of religious abuse across all religious persuasions (Stark & Corcoran, 2014). They provide a collection of horror stories from well-documented accounts in a religious portrait of the world that includes religious persecution and suggestions about why it occurs. They state that "In all, during the past decade there probably have been more than twenty thousand incidents . . . and the total number of deaths probably exceeds three hundred thousand" (Stark & Corcoran, 2014, p. 5). They state that this behavior is certainly not new, and that it is impossible to estimate the number of millions who have died or at least been severely abused as a direct cause of religiously motivated behaviors (Stark & Corcoran, 2014).

Stark and Corcoran (2014) have noted some people's suggestion that one solution to religious abuse might involve a collective means of repression, usually by the state, that produces submission to one church, in which no opposition and therefore no conflict exist. They pointed out that this sort of approach is historically and sociologically naïve and has been proven systemically flawed, having resulted in Europe's religious wars and much of the current violence within Islam. They also have suggested that there is just too much diversity in religious preferences to make such an approach workable. Rather than being a solution, they suggest that such an approach assures an unstable narrowmindedness and would eventually and inevitably result in religiously abusive behaviors (Stark & Corcoran, 2014).

The second possible solution Stark and Corcoran (2014) have identified originates from a form of cultural pluralism, as expounded by one of our nation's founding fathers, Adam Smith (1723–1790):

> Where the society is divided into two of three hundred, or perhaps as many [as a] thousand small sects, of which no one could be considerable enough to disturb the publick tranquility. The teachers of each sect, seeing themselves surrounded on all sides

with more adversaries than friends, would be obliged to learn the candour and moderation which is so seldom to be found among the teachers of great sects. . . . The teachers of each little sect, finding themselves almost alone, would be obliged to respect those of almost every other sect, and the concessions which they would mutually find it both convenient and agreeable to make to one another . . . [would result in] publick tranquility. (Smith, 1776, as cited in Stark & Corcoran, 2014, p. 126)

Building upon the preceding quote, Stark and Corcoran (2014) have stated further,

That is, as each weak religious group seeks to secure itself from attack, self-interest will lead to the collective observance of civility. Put more formally: Where there exist particularistic religions, norms of religious civility will develop to the extent that the society achieves a pluralistic equilibrium. Norms of civility consist of public behavior that is governed by mutual respect among faiths, hence moderation of particularistic commitments in public expressions. A pluralistic equilibrium exists when power is sufficiently diffused among a set of religious bodies so that conflict is not in anyone's interest. (pp. 126, 127)

In this book, Stark and Corcoran (2014) point out that the basic assumption of Smith was that all that is required is a free market wherein the government actions are protective of religious liberty, and underlying this scenario is a neutral and libertarian state. But as these authors point out, that circumstance is commonly not present. They conclude that, although such civility is generally present among American religions, it is likely not exportable unless other nations can find a way to develop civility through years of trial and error (Stark & Corcoran, 2014). Finally, they suggest that the experience of diversity within the United States is not found elsewhere, and therefore not likely to be repeatable, at least not with a subsequent level of civility (p. 130).

In Summary

In this first section of chapter 1, my intention has been to show the relevance of the problem of religious abuse and its importance throughout history. With the hope of finding a better-informed view of recovery, I began by defining religious abuse within a theological context. I then highlighted significant, representative events of religious abuse, placing these occurrences in a cultural context. Finally, I have shown the pervasiveness of religious abuse over all religious traditions, as identified by several historians, theologians, and sociologists. My intent in drawing from these approaches has been to provide a comprehensive, anthropological context and therefore a theoretical benefit for the balance of this paper. The significant and relevant problems caused by religious abuse are clear and must be addressed.

This introductory content leads to the following questions: What possible answers have recently been suggested to address this pervasive problem? And who are the recent dominant and influential writers who offer broad theoretical perspectives within the field of religious abuse and recovery?

As a context for addressing these two questions, Michael Langone (1996) suggested three broad theoretical perspectives: (a) a psychosocial, needs-based understanding, held largely by a variety of professional counselors (Scazzero, 2014; Scazzero & Bird, 2015; Shaw, 2014); (b) a mind-control, victimization point of view, held by many in the cultic-studies milieu (Hassan, 2000, 1988/2015; Lifton, 1961/1989; Lindsey, 2014; Singer & Lalich, 1995; Taylor, 2004); and (c) a Conversionist or deliberative conceptualization, most popular among theologians (Martin, W. & Hanegraaff, H., 1997; Martin, W., 1965/2003) and sociologists (Barker, 1984, 1989; Enroth & Melton, 1985). Additionally, I suggest a fourth perspective for those who follow a (d) dynamic-systems approach, such as that of many in the addictions-recovery/counseling field (Arterburn & Felton, 1991; Johnson, D., & VanVonderen, 1991). I also infer that support for a dynamic-systems viewpoint has come from the field of sociology (Lalich, 2004).

I explore and summarize these perspectives in the second part of this chapter, which follows. This content reflects the stated views and various distinctions that representative authors in the field have suggested in their most influential and significant published works.

Section 2: Recent Literature Review

In the Introduction, I introduced the inherent challenges of understanding religious abuse and recovery, and the general outline of this paper. I addressed the relevance of this topic in the first part of chapter 1, providing an overview of the significant historical occurrences of religious abuse while placing them in our cultural context.

In this second portion of chapter 1, I identify primary and representative literature published over the past fifty-plus years and that reflects four basic theoretical perspectives of religious abuse and recovery. These viewpoints include (a) a *thought-reform or mind-control* understanding, in which one believes that the behavioral dynamics of another's undue influence are the primary causes of a person's involvement in religious abuse; (b) a *deliberative or Conversionist* conceptualization, in which one denies significant undue influence and typically places culpability on the free and varied choices of individual members; (c) a *psychosocial, needs-based* understanding, which suggests that people join, remain in, and exit from religiously abusive environments primarily as the result of their unmet psychological and relational needs; and finally, (d) a *dynamic-systems* approach, which supports the notion that no one influential sphere—imposed/undue influence, deliberated individual choice, or unmet psychological needs—plays a necessary determinative function; instead, an interconnected, dynamic system is essential to understand religious abuse and recovery.

Each of these perspectives has both secular and faith-based adherents. Identified therefore are eight categories of adherents—both secular and faith based, within each of the four major points of view. I begin this review with the early contributors, those viewed as key predecessors, and their most significant contributions, followed by some of their prodigies and their most meaningful publications. I provide a survey of the respective thematic perceptions and the various distinctions among the written works in terms of the basic perspectives.

Thought-Reform/Mind-Control Perspective

The influence of two forebears of the thought-reform/mind-control approach to religious abuse, Robert Lifton and Margaret Thaler Singer, is evident through their most important published contributions. Two more recent writers who are representative of the mind-control perspective and whose principal published contributions have been influential or significant to the current understanding of religious abuse and recovery are Steven Hassan and Paul Martin.

Robert Jay Lifton. A psychiatrist and Distinguished Professor of Psychiatry and Psychology at the John Jay College of Criminal Justice at City University of New York, Robert Jay Lifton conducted significant research on the subject of mind control and thought reform with ex-prisoners of warin

Hong Kong from 1954 to 1955. His research involved multiple, in-depth interviews with forty research subjects (fifteen Chinese and twenty-five Westerners), whose personal experiences as Korean War prisoners were significantly affected by the Chinese Communists' brainwashing attempts. As a direct result of this research, Lifton concluded that thought reform/mind control consists of two basic elements: *confession*, the exposure and renunciation of past and present evil; and *re-education*, the remaking of a man in the image of the manipulator. He stated that these two elements produce a series of pressures and appeals to the intellectual, emotional, and physical being of a person, and that those efforts are aimed at social control and individual change. Lifton is frequently considered the progenitor, or *father* of the thought-reform perspective (Hassan, 2015; Goldberg, L. et al, 2017).

Lifton's primary and most influential writing has been *Thought Reform and the Psychology of Totalism: A Study of Brainwashing in China* (Lifton, 1961/1989). This publication concludes with eight interactive and interconnected psychological themes that, according to Lifton, contribute to the formation of thought reform/mind control (or, as some have described it, ideological totalism). Briefly, these eight key themes are (a) m*ilieu control*—the control of communication within an environment, creating unhealthy boundaries; (b) *mystical manipulation* or "planned spontaneity"—experiences that appear to be spontaneous but are in fact orchestrated to demonstrate "divine authority," which enables the leader(s) to use any means toward a "higher end" or goal; (c) *the demand for purity*—absolute separation of good and evil within the self and within one's environment; (d) *the cult of confession*—one-on-one or group confession of past and present "sins" or behaviors, which are often used to humiliate the confessor and create dependency upon the leadership; (e) *sacred science*—in which the group's teaching is interpreted as ultimate Truth that cannot be questioned; (f) *loading of the language*—in which terms or jargon are used that have group-specific meaning; such phrases will keep one in, or bring one back into the group's mindset; (g) *doctrine over person*—denial of self and self-perception; and finally; (h) *dispensing of existence*—in which anyone not in the group or not embracing the Truth is considered inconsequential, *not saved,* or *unconscious.* This approach results in former members being ostracized or, more generally, the outside world being viewed exceedingly negatively (Lifton, 1961/1989).

Lifton wrote an article and essays (1981, 1987) that connect his prisoner-of-war research and a concise explanation of his eight criteria for defining mind-control involvement to totalitarian forms of religious abuse. Shortly following these articles, he reaffirmed this connection with an updated preface in his *Thought Reform and the Psychology of Totalism: A Study of Brainwashing in China* (1961/1989), the book that researchers and other experts and laypersons interested in in this field refer to extensively for support of a thought-reform/mind-control understanding of religious abuse.

The enduring relevance of Lifton's research is evident in his interview of October 18, 2002, by television personality Bill Moyer, following the September 11, 2001, terror attack (see http://www.pbs.org/now/transcript/transcript_lifton.html). Additionally, in 2006, Lifton, along with fellow psychiatrist Peter A. Olsson, appeared in a documentary on cults, on The History Channel's *Decoding the Past, Cults: Dangerous Devotion: Scholars and Survivors Discuss the Mystery of Cults* (Viswanathan, S., 2009). More recently (September 17, 2016), Lifton was interviewed at length by a leading thought-reform consultant and educator, Steven Hassan (Hassan, 2016).

Margaret Thaler Singer. Whereas Lifton is often treated as progenitor or theoretical father of the concept of the thought-reform and undue-influence perspective, some could easily suggest Margaret Thaler Singer as the pedagogical mother. Margaret Thaler Singer was a clinical psychologist and former Professor Emeritus of the University of California, Berkeley. She previously served on the American Family Foundation (AFF; now International Cultic Studies Association [ICSA]) Board. Singer gave expert testimony in more than two hundred court cases related to religious abuse; played a role in the trial of Kenneth Bianchi in the "Hillside Strangler" case; interviewed more than three thousand former members of religiously abusive environments; was a guest on *PBS Frontline*; was a leading researcher in the field of psychosomatic medicine; and was the first female president of the American Psychosomatic Society, in 1974. She was twice nominated for the Noble Prize for her work in the area of schizophrenia (Psychology Harassment Information Association, n.d.).

Singer's involvement and influence within the field of cultic studies was highly significant, even though her various publications on the topic of religious abuse include only one book. She co-authored this book, *Cults in Our Midst: The Hidden Menace in Our Everyday Lives* (Singer & Lalich, 1995), with Dr. Janja Lalich (discussed later in this chapter), with the forward written by Singer's self-identified mentor and colleague, Robert Jay Lifton. In the book, Singer and Lalich (1995) provided detailed answers to three broad questions about cults:

a. What are *cults*? The authors defined what they meant by cults and provided a brief history (from the 1800s forward). Also included in their discussion is the process of brainwashing, psychological coercion, and thought reform, along with their exposition on the threat and damage of abusive groups.

b. How do they work? Here, the authors suggested the process of recruitment into membership, physiological and psychological persuasion techniques, and how cultsintrude into the workplace and intimidate.

c. How can we help survivors to escape and recover? Here, Singer and Lalich (1995) reiterated much of Lifton's contributions to the cultic-studies field.

They reframed the eight interactive/interconnected behavioral themes Lifton identified as necessary for thought reform, reducing them to six social conditions necessary for thought reform to be effective:

i. Keep the person unaware that there is an agenda to control or change the person.

ii. Control time and physical environment (contacts, information).

iii. Create a sense of powerlessness, fear, and dependency.

iv. Suppress old behavior and attitudes.

v. Instill new behavior and attitudes.

vi. Put forth a closed system of logic. (Singer & Lalich, p. 64)

However, as with most significant literary works, the ideas expressed in this book (Singer & Lalich, 1995) did not come from a vacuum but were built upon other published works and experience. This book grew from prior important articles by Singer, including her earliest and most well-known, "Coming Out of the Cults" (1979); "Thought Reform Programs and the Production of Psychiatric Casualties" (1990); "Undue Influence and Written Documents: Psychological Aspects" (1992); a co-authored article with Margaret Singer, Maurice Temerlin, and Michael Langone, "Psychotherapy Cults" (1990), and many other co-authored articles published primarily in the *Cultic Studies Journal*.

Other notable thought-reform professionals. In addition to the work and influence of Lifton and Singer, a number of other professionals in the field who fall within the general thought-reform perspective can easily be identified: David Clark (1998); Carol Giambalvo (1996 [co-author, Herbert

Rosedale]); Steven Hassan (2000, 2012, 2015); Paul Martin (1989, 1999); and relative newcomers Wendy Duncan (2006); Luna Lindsey (2014); and Kathleen Taylor (2004). Of these, perhaps the most representative, influential, or significant contributions that support a thought-reform perspective are from Steven Hassan (2000, 2012, 1988/2015); and Paul Martin (1989, 1999). Hassan, whom I will cover first, self-identifies as coming from a secular approach, followed by Martin, who adhered to a faith-based (Christian) viewpoint.

Steven Hassan. A member of the Unification Church (commonly referred to as the Moonies) from 1974 to 1976, Hassan has since worked in the cultic-studies field for forty-plus years, assisting others in their recovery from abusive and controlling environments. He is now an educator and licensed mental health counselor; he has described himself in various ways, including "America's Best-Known Cult Expert" (Hassan, 1988/2015). He provides thought-reform intervention services and is often found in the media spotlight. His most relevant and influential publications are *Combating Cult Mind Control* (1988/2015); *Releasing the Bonds: Empowering People to Think for Themselves* (2000); and *Freedom of Mind: Helping Loved Ones Leave Controlling People, Cults and Beliefs* (2012). *Releasing the Bonds* (2000) and *Freedom of Mind* (2012) contain the theoretic groundwork for the most current edition of *Combatting Cult Mind Control* (1988/2016).

In *Combatting Cult Mind Control,* Hassan (1988/2015) identifies the Strategic Interactive Approach (SIA) as his own perspective of recovery from mind-control influences. He states that he believes his approach is "customized, sophisticated, a complex systems-theory approach, whereby I create a unique and ethical influence campaign to help individuals acquire a set of experiences and realizations that help them remove many of the invisible chains of mind control" (p. 25). Throughout this book, Hassan primarily emphasizes the deception, manipulation, and indoctrination that people experience within the closed system of obedience and dependency found within religiously and politically abusive environments. He places clear emphasis on what has *happened to* the individual—undue influence, rather than the individual's culpability for choices made, or family history. According to Hassan, the intervention goal is to assist the former victim of religious abuse to "get back in touch with their real selves" (p. 241). Hassan states the need for three short-term objectives: (a) build rapport and trust, (b) gather information, and (c) plant seeds of doubt about the religiously abusive group while promoting a new perspective (p. 242). In chapter 10,

Hassan suggests eight basic keys to "unlocking mind control": (a) "Build rapport and trust"; (b) "Use goal-oriented communication"; (c) "Develop models of identity"; (d) Put the persons in touch with their real identities; (e) Get the cult members "to look at reality from many different perspectives"; (f) "Sidestep the thought-stopping process by giving information in an indirect way"; (g) Help the persons "visualize a happy future outside" their abusive group; and finally, (h) "Offer the . . . member[s] concrete definitions of mind control and specific characteristics of a destructive" group (pp. 247–48).

In addition to the prolific and well-known Steven Hassan (1988/2015), who strongly supports Lifton and Singer's secular thought-reform/mind-control perspectives, many others come from a faith-based orientation (Clark, D., 1998; Duncan, 2006; Enroth, 1992, 1994; Martin, P., 1989, 1990, 1993a, 1998, 1999, 2000). Each of these writers self-identifies as Christian and appeals to a Christian worldview as found in the Bible as a foundational support for their positions. Dr. Paul Martin was a key contributor among this group.

Paul Martin. Dr. Martin was a former member of the Great Commission Association of Churches (GCAC), sometimes identified as the Great Commission International (GCI) or Great Commission Churches (GCC). For many years, GCC was identified as an abusive, controlling organization of Christian churches (Enroth, 1992). Paul Martin was a practicing psychologist and the founder of one of the first short-term, inpatient treatment centers for those who had suffered religious abuse and were in need of recovery. Wellspring Retreat Center in Athens, Ohio was founded in 1986. Since Martin's death (2009), Wellspring continues primarily as a mental-health, outpatient treatment service for former members of religiously abusive environments, with Greg Sammons as its executive director (see http://wellspringretreat.org).

Paul Martin published many articles, some of which are "Post-Cult Rehabilitation Counseling" (*Wellspring Messenger*, 1990); "Post-Cult Recovery: Assessment and Rehabilitation" (Langone, M., 1993a); "Wellspring's Approach to Cult Rehab" (1993b); "Overcoming the Bondage of Revictimization: A Rational/Empirical Defense of Thought Reform," co-authored with Lawrence Pile, Ron Burks, and Stephen Martin (1998); "Toxic Faith or Thought Reform," part 1 (1999) and part 2 (2000). He also was the author of the book *Cult Proofing Your Kids* (1993c).

Paul Martin's most significant and representative publications in the literature from the mind-control perspective for understanding religious abuse and recovery include an article and a book. He wrote "Dispelling the Myths: The Psychological Consequences of Cultic Involvement" (1989), his first published article on the subject, for one of the largest and most well-known Christian journals, *Christian Research Journal*. This article offers two illustrative stories of religious abuse and failed attempts at recovery. In it, Martin discussed six myths that are commonly attributed to individuals' involvement in religiously abusive environments:

a.   Myth #1: Ex-cult members do not have psychological problems. Their problems are wholly spiritual.

b.   Myth #2: Ex-cult members do have psychological disorders. But these people have come from clearly non-Christian cults.

c.   Myth #3: Both Christian and non-Christian groups can produce problems, but all of the people involved [in the groups] must have had prior psychological hang-ups that would have surfaced regardless of what group they joined.

d.   Myth #4: While normal unbelievers [Christian] may get involved with cults, born-again believers will not. And even if they did, their involvement would not affect them so negatively.

e.   Myth #5: Christians can and do get involved in these aberrational groups and they can get hurt emotionally. But all they really need is some good Bible teaching and a warm, caring Christian fellowship and they will be fine.

f.   Myth #6: Perhaps the best way for these ex-members to receive help is to see a professional therapist such as a psychologist, psychiatrist, or mental health counselor. (p. 8)

Cult Proofing Your Kids (Martin, 1993c) is Paul Martin's only published book. In this book, Martin built upon his first article (Martin, 1989), providing suggestions for the reader about the definition of a religiously abusive environment, how to spot one, and why people join them. In the book, Martin (1993c) denies the importance of thoughtful decision-making about doctrine content and prefers other reasons for why people join a religiously abusive group: (a) "healing for emotional hurts" (p. 41), (b) "establishing friendships and relationships" (p. 44), and (c) "spiritual growth" (p. 45) along with the issue of mind control (see pp. 39, 92, 172). Martin strongly emphasizes the importance of understanding Lifton's principles of thought reform, or mind control (see pp. 185–90). And because of this prominence, Martin's approach and writings most consistently reflect a mind-control perspective.

Advocates for the thought-reform/mind-control perspective believe it is primarily the behavioral dynamics of another's undue influence that cause a person's involvement in and consequent needed recovery from religious abuse. Culpability is predominantly laid upon the manipulative nature of the abusive group or person(s) in question. Recovery is primarily found through education about mind-control dynamics and their application to the relational environment in question. Those professionals identified as coming primarily from this viewpoint have either a secular or religious orientation, with most presenting as secular in their conceptualizations. Advocates for both secular and faith-based perspectives, however, make strong primary appeals to the theoretical work of Lifton (1961/1989) and of Singer and Lalich (1995).

Deliberative or Conversionist Perspective

An alternate perspective within the literature that addresses religious abuse and recovery strongly opposes the thought-reform view, instead reflecting the view that autonomous choices of the individual are foundational to understanding the cause of religious abuse. This Conversionist understanding, as with the mind-control perspective, is founded upon both a secular and religious (Christian) viewpoint.

Those individuals with a secular orientation typically have a strong sociological background and often claim to be value-neutral. Many are strongly defensive of questionable groups, both in their writing and in their court testimonials. Commonly in the literature, those in this secular group are referred to as *cult apologists*, *cult sympathizers*, or simply *procult* (see Langone, 1995, pp. *xvi*, 29–35). I begin this review of the Conversionist literature by examining two early spokespersons: Eileen Barker, from the secular perspective, and Walter Martin, from the religious (Christian) point of view.

Eileen Barker. Professor Barker has been a prolific secular author in the field of religious abuse from the Conversionist point of view. As Professor Emeritus of Sociology, London School of Economics at the University of London, she has more than three hundred and fifty professional publications in her name on the topic of religious experience, and she has frequently been a court advocate for various religious groups that some believe are abusive. In 1988, Professor Barker founded the Information Network Focus on Religious Movement (INFORM), an independent, informational charity supported by the British government and mainstream UK churches for the purpose of providing accurate, balanced, and current factual information about alternative religious, spiritual, and esoteric movements. INFORM is based at the London School of Economics. I consider Barker's two most quoted books (1984, 1995) in the following paragraphs.

In her award-winning book *The Making of a Moonie—Brainwashing of Choice?* (Barker, 1984), Barker described her academic research findings related to her seven-year personal experience of the Unification Church and the "Moonies." She stated that most in the media and the general public wrongfully suggest that brainwashing, mind control, or thought techniques were used to elicit membership in the Unification Church (pp. 1–3).

Barker described her research and the methodology she used to collect and analyze empirical data in the United Kingdom and the United States in the formulation of this book (Barker, 1984, pp. 12–37). She addressed the issue of purported brainwashing, concluding that she saw no evidence of adherents being passive victims of forces beyond their control, and that she witnessed no mental coercion within the organization. She acknowledged the presence of some environmental controls, deception, and the practice of *love-bombing* (an initial period in which members offered an inordinate amount of positive attention to potential members in their recruitment efforts). Her primary appeal in the book was to credit members' previous life experiences and personal disposition in accounting for why some individuals are attracted to the Unification Church and most are not. She stated that, counter to the theory that thought reform/mind control accounts for membership to the Unification Church, we should instead view involvement as a natural suggestibility and susceptibility of those who choose to join. She contended that this inclination is based on one's social conditioning and personal selection, on a "rational-choice pole of the continuum rather than ... to the irresistible brainwashing pole" (Barker, 1984, p. 250–51). Throughout the book, Barker stated that, contrary to any thought-reform/mind-control influence, those who join are not passive responders. She claimed that people who join the Unification Church are instead active agents seeking to fulfill religious longings and fulfillment of relational needs, primarily by their own, uninhibited, decision-making process.

Unlike *The Making of a Moonie*, Barker's second book, *New Religious Movements: A Practical Introduction* (1995), goes beyond academic research and interest. In it, she strongly affirmed the practical human need to understand involvement in groups, which some view as damaging. She referred to these groups, most of which she noted had emerged since the 1950s, as *new religious movements (NRMs)*. In this framing, and contrary to those affirming a mind-control perspective, she professed to have a greater value-neutral stance toward NRMs. She acknowledged that "It is, of course, well-nigh impossible to be completely objective and value-free" (p. x); she also stated that "social science is in itself [value] neutral" (p. xi). She expressed her belief that purported damage by NRMs is greatly exaggerated.

As in her first book (1984), in *New Religious Movements* (1995) Barker reiterated a denial of mind control, which she has defined as a lack of free agency in decision making. In this book she affirmed her belief that understanding involvement in NRMs and avoiding confusion ultimately requires going beyond a group's contributions to consider the individual's personality, personal history, hopes, fears, and, most importantly, deliberative decision making. She denied any significant uniqueness in one's involvement in an NRM compared to any other social system such as family, school, the military, or traditional religion. She professed to have greater academic objectivity about NRMs than do supporters of the mind-control perspective, and she appealed to the positive experiences of NRM membership. She included among such experiences growth of a strong work ethic, which would lead eventually to improved career development; enhancement of meditation or mindfulness techniques and changed diet, which would result in improved health and longevity; increased community involvement, which would offer social and relational benefits; increased experience of personal discipline and life commitment, which would result in enhanced self-development; and ample opportunities to discuss religious questions, which would in turn lead to one being better informed about religious matters. Like others coming from a secular perspective, Barker affirmed the importance of *deed over creed* in a spiritual community, and a community in which issues of religious orthodoxy are discounted or minimized as determinersof the group's health.

Unlike their secular counterpart, those who hold to a strong religious (Christian) perspective within a Conversionist approach affirm *creed over deed* for determining the value or health of the group being considered, and they see issues of orthodoxy as paramount. These faith-based adherents are typically researchers, theologians, pastors, and professors at religious institutions; they often are referred to as *countercult apologists*, or simply *anticult*

(Langone, 1995, pp. xvi, 29–35). Those in this group use theological arguments to make their perspectives known. Of the faith-based contributors holding to this Conversionist viewpoint, two stand out as most influential and significant in their contributions: Walter Martin and Hank Hanegraaff.

Walter Martin. An ordained American Baptist minister with a doctoral degree, Walter Martin is considered by many Evangelicals the most influential father figure within the current field of countercult apologetics. In 1960, he founded and directed the parachurch Evangelical Christian Research Institute (CRI) (see https://www.theopedia.com/walter-martin). Many similar secular and faith-based informational clearinghouses provide the public with researched facts on religious and New Age beliefs and practices, but Christian Research Institute is the largest, most influential, and oldest of its kind. CRI also publishes the *Christian Research Journal.* This popular monthly magazine addresses Christian doctrine (belief), Christian defense (apologetics), and discernment (culticstudies; see http://www.equip.org/christian-research-journal).

Dr. Martin's extensive writings included many books, articles, and educational pamphlets. Chief and most influential of his writing is *The Kingdom of the Cults* (Martin, W., 1965/2003). This publication has seen many revisions, updates, and expansions. Using the most recent edition, I explore and identify its influence and relevance to this paper in the following paragraphs.

This text (Martin, W., 1965/2003) provides a survey of information and comparative evaluation of numerous religious groups and their systems of belief (e.g., Christian Science, Jehovah's Witnesses, Mormonism, Armstrongism, Scientology, Theosophy, the Unification Church, Islam, Buddhism, Seventh-day Adventism). Dr. Martin compared and contrasted Christianity with the beliefs and practices of various groups. Since Dr. Martin's death in 1989, people who were strongly influenced by his life and work (daughter, Jill Martin Rische, and her husband Kevin Rische; popular and well-known Christian apologist Ravi Zacharias, and Hank Hanegraaff, the current President and Chairman of the Board of CRI) have been responsible for updating and revising of this text.

The focus throughout *The Kingdom of the Cults* (Martin, W., 1965/2003) is the importance of well-informed education concerning various religious belief systems. Readers are encouraged to take seriously their Christian faith for their own benefit, and to evangelize those of contrary beliefs. The importance of the deity of Christ, His death and resurrection, and the reliability of the Bible (both Old Testament and New Testament) are themes throughout this text. In chapter 3, "The Psychological Structure of Cultism," Dr. Martin identified three consistently common psychologically driven features of cultic patterns. The first and most influential facet is the experience of having one's worldview forcefully defined by another. The second feature includes the authority imposed upon and accepted by the member, thus determining one's larger-life decision making. The third feature involves a penetrating dynamic that controls the structure of everyday living.

Dr. Martin used the term *brainwashing* or equivalent (*thought reform* or *mind control*) only once in this text (Martin, W., 1965, p. 36), and he did not define or link it in any way to Lifton or Singer and their perspectives on mind control. It appears that, as a theologian, teacher, apologist, and preacher, Dr. Martin's foundational answer to countering religious abuse and acquiring recovery from what he termed *cults* involved theological education that results in one's acceptance of a mainline, orthodox Christian perspective. In other words, Martin believed that responding to religious abuse primarily requires countering false beliefs and the positive acceptance of the truth claims of historic Christianity. His position on the significance of the biblical scriptures as corrective and reparative is evidenced by an extensive, thirteen-page Scripture Index at the end of his book (Martin, W., 2003).

Walter Martin influenced many, particularly within the Evangelical community, to accept a faith-based, Conversionist approach to understanding religious abuse. Many Christian countercult apologists attribute their life's ministry efforts directly and substantially to having been shaped by Dr. Martin.

Hank Hanegraaff. Another influential author in the Conversionist perspective and heavily influenced by Walter Martin is Hank Hanegraaff, Martin's close associate replacement as the current president and Chairman of the Board at CRI. Like his predecessor, Hanegraaff's views on religiously abusive groups are primarily defined and therefore shaped by a faith-based Conversionist approach to understanding religiously abusive systems. Upon Martin's death, Hanegraaff assumed not only Martin's CRI role, but replaced him as his heir apparent in the popular, nationally syndicated, radio talk show, the *Bible Answer Man*. As one deeply committed to intellectually equipping Christians to discern between theological orthodoxy and counterfeits, Hanegraaff is the author or editor of more than twenty related books, and an outspoken and controversial figure within the Christian countercult movement. Despite the lack of a college degree and his responsibilities as the father of twelve children, he has become a major influence in the cultic-studies field.

Hanegraaff was the general editor of Walter Martin's revised and expanded edition of *The Kingdom of the Cults* (1997), in which he suggested a theological grid to determine the level of credibility and therefore health of a religious system (as previously discussed). In addition to his contributions to this modern-day classic (Martin, W., 1965/2003), Hanegraaff's most pertinent publications related to the topic of religious abuse and recovery are *Counterfeit Revival* (2001) and *Christianity in Crisis* (2012). In these works, he has addressed what he sees as theological distortions that result in manipulative forms of abuse within Christendom.

Specifically, in *The Counterfeit Revival* (2001), Hanegraaff suggested that modern-day Christianity is undergoing a dramatic shift away from authentic faith, facts, and reason and moving toward hyped-up feelings, fantasy, and esoteric revelation, which have led to widespread abuses within many churches. In this context, he identified several influential church leaders: Rodney Howard Browne, Charismatic Christian preacher and evangelist (pp. 22–29); John Arnott, Toronto Airport Vineyard Pastor (pp. 46–56); Paul Cain, a modern-day prophet (pp. 173–74); and William Marrion Branham, one of "the most revered leaders of today's Counterfeit Revival" (p. 150). Hanegraaff believes that, as the result of heretical church teaching, many members are emotionally manipulated, fraudulent claims are imposed, and magical thinking is encouraged, with disastrous results. The needful corrective, according to Hanegraaff, is acknowledging the truth behind historic Christian beliefs based on a clear understanding of biblical teaching regarding authentic spirituality and experience.

Hanegraaff has reiterated his Conversionist approach in his more recent book, *Christianity in Crisis* (2012). In it, he identified the Word of Faith movement, also commonly referred to as The Health and Wealth Gospel, which claims that Christians can experience perfect health and abounding wealth if only they exercise the right kind of faith. This movement originated in the late twentieth century, primarily through Pentecostal and Charismatic churches. Hanegraaff specifically addresses five representative and influential preachers active in the Word of Faith movement. He stated that Word of Faith teachers present a false view of the Bible and Christian spirituality, which has resulted in numerous abuses. He posited that the remedy to religious abuse comes by better decision making based on information found in what the Bible teaches, a conclusion that supports a perspective consistent with a Conversionist understanding of religious abuse.

Both religious and secular proponents within the Conversionist viewpoint place a particular emphasis on the importance of education, as both a preventative inoculation and a foundation for recovery following religious abuse. Both groups of proponents place primary culpability for membership in religiously abusive environments upon the free and varied choices of individual adherents. Within the broader perspective of this approach, two very divergent conceptualizations are evident, one primarily secular and one religious. Within the religious contingent, theological arguments are commonly used to frame and defend that perspective.

Secular Psychosocial/Needs-Based Perspective

As with both the Conversionist approach and the mind-control viewpoint, the psychosocial, needs-based perspective has early influencers and more recent researchers and writers. I start with one such forebear who has contributed much to the field. I then identify other, more recent authors whose writing distinguishes their views. Finally, I identify the main contributions by these authors to this field. Some writers come from a secular orientation and others primarily from a religious frame of reference. I begin with three secular representatives, followed with two whose viewpoints are religious (Christian).

Michael Langone. A psychologist since 1979, Dr. Langone has counseled with several hundred former members and their families who have experienced religious abuse. Since 1981, Langone has been the Executive Director of the ICSA, the largest and most well-known global network of people concerned about psychological manipulation by those from controlling/abusive environments. ICSA is a 501c3 nonprofit educational organization primarily comprising professional clinicians, social workers, educators, researchers, thought-reform consultants and a broad mix of other individuals negatively affected by undue influence or control.

Similar to the voluminous Eileen Barker, Langone has been both a prolific author and editor in the literature of religious abuse and recovery. Most of his publications have been under the auspices of the ICSA and its predecessor the AFF; but he also has authored and co-authored numerous articles in professional journals and books. Because of both the sheer volume of his numerous publications and their respective value, it is challenging to select his most significant contributions. With that caveat, I consider two of Langone's publishing efforts, *Recovery From Cults: Help for Victims of Psychological and Spiritual Abuse* (Langone, 1993), and *Cult Recovery: A Clinician's Guide* (Goldberg, L., Goldberg, W., Henry, R., & Langone, M., 2017).

In *Recovery From Cults* (1993), Langone is both an author (along with twenty-two others) and the book's editor. The various contributors include mental health practitioners, investigative journalists, clergy, law-enforcement personnel, lawyers, a medical doctor, and various educators. Most of these writers have at least one book in print, and many have written multiple professional journal articles that address their particular areas of interest related to abuse in controlling groups and abusive religious systems.

The central focus of *Recovery From Cults* (1993) is "to help former members of cults and related groups, their families, and helping professionals increase their understanding of the post-cult recovery process" (p. 1). Principles are provided to help readers understand cult conversion, along with postcult problems and recovery. The authors accomplish this by drawing from psychological literature related to thought reform, commonly known as brainwashing; clinical reports by psychotherapists and pastoral counselors; and finally, from the many clinical experiences of the book's various contributors. This text provides an overview of religious abuse and recovery and primarily affirms a mind-control or thought-reform perspective.

Fast-forward twenty-four years to 2017, and, as coeditor, Michael Langone again lends his editorial acumen, experience, and knowledge to one of the newest, comprehensive, published works on this important topic (Goldberg, L. et al., 2017). Unlike the broad appeal of the first publication (Langone, 1993), this 2017 text, with twenty-one specialized chapters from twenty-two different authors, was written specifically with the intent of providing specific guidelines for mental health professionals who may work with former members of religiously abusive environments, and their families. Langone (Goldberg, L. et al., 2017) again provides the reader with the Introduction to this text and a chapter overview for the subsection of chapters focused on special issues and recent research. The significance of this publication is that it offers readers multiple resources and perspectives for understanding religious abuse and recovery, primarily from a psychosocial/needs-based vantage point. Some of the previous authors from *Recovery From Cults* (Langone, 1993) are included in *Cult Recovery* (Goldberg, L. et al., 2017), but many are not, and others have been added. Absent from *Cult Recovery* is the Preface from a decidedly thought-reform author, Margaret Singer in *Recovery From Cults* (Singer, M., 1993). Absent also is the mind-control emphasis, with the predominant theme of psycho-social needs in its place. Both books were written under ICSA leadership and control. Perhaps seeking to account for the change in emphasis in these two important co-authored works, Langone includes the following in his introductory comments in *Cult Recovery*:

> I have written about three models of cult recruitment (Langone, 1996): The *deliberative* model says that people join because of what they think about the group. The *psychodynamic* model says that people join because of what the group does for them (e.g., meets unconscious psychological needs). The *thought-reform* model says that people join because of what the group does to them (i.e., manipulation). All three models probably play a role in most cult conversions. Hence, observers who are rigidly partial to one or another of the models may not fully understand a particular cultic conversion. (p. xx)

Langone has made broad and deep contributions to the cultic-studies field. These contributions include facilitating cooperation among a variety of other contributors to this topic, encouraging their unique offerings in this important field of study; supporting the distribution of publications of numerous individuals through various worldwide venues; challenging those who might otherwise not be inclined to work together; and providing significant educational opportunities in his management of ICSA's many national and international conferences. In addition, Langone's various re-search projects and written contributions have added insight and direction to the general field of cultic studies.

While Langone has indeed contributed much to the broad field of cultic-studies, many others' works coming from the secular psychosocial/needs-based perspective also deserve recognition: Doni Whitsett (2017); Lorna Goldberg (1993; 2017a; 2017b); William Goldberg (1993; 2017a; 2017b; 2017c); and more recently contributing within this arena, Daniel Shaw (2014; 2017) and Gillie Jenkinson (2017). In the following para-graphs, I discuss two authors from among those presenting from a secular approach who may well be considered most representative, influential, and significant within the psychosocial/needs-based perspective.

Daniel Shaw. A psychoanalyst in private practice in New York City and Nyack, New York, Daniel Shaw is Faculty and Clinical Supervisor at the National Institute for the Psychotherapies (NIP); Clinical Supervisor and faculty member at Westchester Center for the Study of Psychoanalysis and Psychotherapy, New York; Adjunct Clinical Supervisor at Smith College of Social Work, Massachusetts, and, as noted, a relative newcomer to the field of cultic studies. He has thirteen years of personal religious-abuse history as a past staff member in Siddha Yoga, SYDA Foundation, from which he exited in 1994. With Chris Carlson, Shaw now coleads the monthly New York area ICSA abuse-recovery support group. This group provides support, education, and interaction for those who have been harmed by or want to learn about abusive organizations (see http://www.icsahome.com/ elibrary/peopleprofiles).

Shaw is included among the twenty-two authors of *Cult Recovery: A Clinician's Guide to Working with Former Members and Families* (Shaw 2017, pp. 395–412). In his earlier substantive publication, *Traumatic Narcissism: Relational Systems of Subjugation* (2014), Shaw frames his perspective of religious abuse around the developmental needs of the individual and "the relational system of the traumatizing narcissist [religiously abusive leader(s)]" (p. xiv). Here, he stated that the "The traumatizing narcissist seeks to abolish intersubjectivity and to freeze a complementary dynamic in the relationship, allowing recognition in one direction only—toward himself" (p. xv). He believes that this traumatic narcissism evidenced in the leadership of religiously abusive systems "is a particular form of attachment-related trauma" (p. 18). More broadly, he states that "humans have objectified, enslaved, and dehumanized other humans" because of traumatizing narcissism (p. 58).

Shaw's two concepts of applying *analytic love* and supporting *self-differentiation* of clients are essential values to religious-abuse recovery. Analytic love involves the counselors' ability to do their work with self-awareness, acknowledging their own vulnerability, fallibility, and shame based-beliefs and behaviors in the process. Clinicians must be able to employ this capability while protecting both the integrity of their therapeutic efforts and the interpsychic and relational needs of their clients. According to Shaw, addressing the past relational wounds through insight-directed counseling encourages clients to work with issues of forgiveness, hatred, and indifference; develop the ability to bear past pain; eventually find healthy and sincere religious devotion; and develop the capacity for self-sacrifice to achieve relational emancipation or improved self-differentiation. In the process of expressing his psychoanalytic approach to trauma-based abuses, whether evidenced in a therapeutic setting or in an abusive religious system, Shaw

38

supports the perspective of a psychosocial/needs-based understanding as a primary requirement for one to understand religious abuse and recovery.

Doni Whitsett. Like Dan Shaw, Doni Whitsett, a Clinical Professor at the USC Suzanne Dworak-Peck School of Social Work in Los Angeles, and a secular proponent of the secular psychosocial/needs-based perspective, supports a psychosocial/needs-based approach to the issue of religious abuse and affirms the importance of the therapeutic relationship. Coming from a psychodynamic orientation, Whitsett offers a double-helix model that "deals with both conscious and unconscious forces, and past and present phenomena" (Whitsett, 2017, p. 193). She teaches various classes on practice, behavior, mental health, and human sexuality. Whitsett has worked with those from religiously abusive environments and their families for twenty-plus years, and she lectures on topics related to cultic studies. She has presented at conferences nationally and internationally, specifically on the topics of trauma and self-psychology as they relate to religious abuse and recovery. Her most recent publishing contribution (Goldberg, L. et al., 2017, chapter 9) is representative of her perspective on understanding and recovery from religious abuse.

In this significant chapter (Goldberg et al., 2017, chapter 9), Whitsett conceptualizes her view of the recovery needs of former members of religiously abusive groups as psychodynamic in character. Early in the chapter, she stresses the importance of the therapeutic relationship, and of producing an empathic holding environment in the context of counseling those with past trauma related to religious abuse. Building on Freudian concepts of the role of the unconscious, transference, and conflict, along with Freud's ideas of coping and defensive functioning, she acknowledges the importance of internal-object relationships and early attachment patterns. Recognizing the influence of past significant attachment figures and their impact leads Whitsett to conceive of a *double-helix model* (pp. 192–94) related to recovery from religious abuse. Although she acknowledges that her model has been suggested by other theorists (Wilkinson, 2010), it has not been directly applied before to working with former members who have experienced religious abuse.

According to Whitsett, this psychodynamic approach involves the thoughtful therapeutic weaving of the two strands or paths of building a present life and working through the religious-abuse trauma. As the client is ready, Whitsett suggests that the counselor work alternatively between these two therapeutic themes. A third connective strand, the compassionate therapeutic relationship, makes the process effectual. As Whitsett states, this is a "psychodynamic approach because it deals with both conscious and unconscious forces, and past and present phenomena" (Whitsett, 2017, p. 193). She explains that, to counter unhelpful projections from occurring frequently with former members, the therapist should be more active and directive, rather than passive and nondirective. This approach provides a safe place in which the clients' trauma can be processed and eventually integrated into their internal understanding of self. Further, building critical-thinking skills and enhanced ego functioning, modifying dysfunctional ego defenses, and focusing on self-differentiating identity issues are all goals for recovery. Psychoeducation plays an important role in providing enhanced critical-thinking skills and the integration of dissociated memories.

Likewise, according to Whitsett (2017), the creation of a timeline, from when one joined the religiously abusive environment to the exit of the same, and understanding mind-control dynamics as they are applied to the client's particular group, are important features of this approach. Assisting the religiously abused person in gaining an understanding of how the experiences of their past affects the present helps them work through past trauma. This process includes their religious-abuse history and family of origin, if those are one and the same. The dynamic relationship between client and therapist encourages a secure attachment bond that helps counter the previous unhealthy traumatic attachments clients experienced in the religiously abusive system. Finally, in the implementation of the first strand of the double-helix model, building a present life; of the second, working through trauma; and enabled by the third, the secure therapeutic relationship, a new, healthy, coconstructed life can appear for the client.

Religious Psychosocial Perspective

Similar to those holding a secular psychosocial viewpoint, many authors frame their approach to this basic worldview within a religious (Christian) conceptualization in their understanding of religious abuse and recovery. Two significant contributors come from such a religious psychosocial perspective.

Robert Pardon and Judy Pardon. Robert and Judy Pardon are a married team who have contributed much to the literature and practice to increase our understanding in the field of religious abuse and recovery. To this partnership, Judy brings twenty years of teaching and a counseling background, while Robert brings fifteen years' experience of having been a Christian pastor. Both are directors of the New England Institute of Religious Research (NEIRR), founded in 1991. As an information clearinghouse, NEIRR provides concerned individuals and organizations with current research on religiously abusive groups, along with activities that bring emotional and spiritual healing for former members (see http://neirr. org/instte.html). As a natural extension of NEIRR came a unique long-term (up to twelve months) residential rehabilitation facility, MeadowHaven (see http://www.meadowhaven.org). Founded in 2002 as a nonprofit organization, MeadowHaven is located in Lakeville Massachusetts. MeadowHaven's unique mission is to assist those who have experienced significant religious emotional or physical abuse and are in need of recovery. Over the past 10 years, the Pardons have specialized in Bible-based communal and aberrational Christian groups, helping former members from such groups to rebuild their lives.

In addition to their work at MeadowHaven, the Pardons are often consulted by law enforcement regarding destructive groups, and they provide expert legal witness testimony. Both Robert and Judy have spoken many times nationally and internationally concerning their work at MeadowHaven, and in 2014 they received ICSA's prestigious Herbert L. Rosedale Award (see www.icsahome.com/aboutus/awards). In late 2017, the Pardons contributed "Residential Treatment Modality for Cult Trauma Survivors," chapter 17 in ICSA's *Cult Recovery* handbook (Pardon, R., & Pardon J., 2017) discussed previously. The Pardons have outlined their work at MeadowHaven and their contributions to the field of recovery from religious abuse in this chapter, recapped in the following paragraphs.

After a brief introduction to the significance of the psychological features of religious abuse as identified in many well-known occurrences, the Pardons provide an overview of MeadowHaven's approach to religious-abuse recovery. They state that treatment at MeadowHaven is both "phenomenologically driven and eclectic in nature" (Pardon, R., & Pardon, J., 2017, p. 368). The therapy offered commonly includes intense and individual counseling, support-group meetings, relevant video clips, homework, and individualized psychodynamic exercises. The authors intentionally refer to their clientele as *residents*, rather than *patients* or *clients*. They do this to subtly shift their residents' self-perceptions from victims to active participants in the healing process. The goal in the program is rehabilitation, not conversion to a particular religious belief. The Pardons view communication as the eventual need of each individual to "dismantle the belief system that fueled all their abuse, then let go of the evil parts and hold on to the good" (2017, p. 371). The staff at MeadowHaven, similar to the staff at Wellspring, come from a Christian worldview and likewise are very careful not to apply pressure regarding their belief systems. But unlike with a secular approach, they do not avoid religious beliefs. The MeadowHaven program (http://www.meadowhaven.org/program.html) is "loosely based on Judith Herman's [trauma] treatment model (Herman, 2015)" as

> a three-phased approach that moves from stabilization and edu-cation (Resting and Safety); to deconditioning of the traumatic, cult-based events, memories, and overwhelming emotions with positive, personal reframing (Remembering and Mourning); to future focus and personal goals, and creating safe social connec-tions and meaningful activities (Reconnecting). (Pardon, R., & Pardon, J., 2017, p. 372)

The authors clearly describe and illustrate these three recovery phases with specific case examples.

The Pardons' approach at MeadowHaven consists of three frequently communicated core principles: "There is nothing wrong with you. Rather, there was something done to you that has created the issues that brought you here. . . . You cannot change what you do not understand. . . . You can-not change what you do not [personally] own" (Pardon, R., & Pardon, J., 2017, p. 373).

The Pardons then articulate in their chapter lessons they learned in the course of their work at MeadowHaven: (a) the importance of "better initial assessments"; (b) "more awareness of resident dependency issues"; and (c) the need for a "wider network of extended support" (Pardon, R., & Pardon, J., 2017, pp. 386–87). Their unique contributions to the field of recovery from religious abuse strongly support the importance of work-ing through damaging belief systems. The Pardons are an example of how combined writing efforts (with decidedly different educational and experi-ence backgrounds) can result in significant contributions to the study of religious abuse and recovery.

Whether secular or religious, the psychosocial/needs-based approach to religious abuse and recovery suggests that people join, remain in, and exit religiously abusive environments primarily because of their own un-met psychological and relational needs and that, at varying levels, people are mutually culpable for their involvement. Most of those holding this core belief come from the general field of counseling and psychology.

Secular Dynamic-Systems Perspective

In addition to the three broad perspectives presented to this point, I now consider literature that supports the fourth general viewpoint: a dynamic-systems perspective. As previously mentioned, this point of view affirms much of what is present within the prior three approaches, but it also adds an important systemic and comprehensive component to involvement in and recovery from religiously abusive environments. Foundationally, no one influential sphere—psychological need, imposed influence, or deliberate individual choice—plays a necessary determinative role; instead, a variable and interconnected dynamic system is essential to fully understand and treat religious abuse. Those who adhere to this viewpoint, as with each of the previously discussed perspectives, are identifiable through their most significant writing. Three noteworthy contributors to the topic of religious abuse and recovery who write from this perspective include Janja Lalich, who has primarily been informed by a secular orientation (Lalich, 2004, 2006 [with Madeleine Tobias], 2018 [with Karla McLaren]), and David Johnson along with Jeff VanVonderen, who write from a religious (Christian) point of view (Johnson & VanVonderen, 1991).

Janja Lalich. A Professor Emerita of Sociology at California State University Chico, Janja Lalich has thirty-plus years of research, writing, and speaking experience on the topic of cultic studies. Her website biography reads in part as follows:

> [She] is a researcher, author, and educator specializing in cults and extremist groups, with a particular focus on charismatic relationships, political and other social movements, ideology and social control, and issues of gender and sexuality. She has been a consultant to educational, mental health, business, media, and legal professionals, as well as having worked with current members, former members, and families of members of controversial groups. (Lalich, n.d.)

In addition to the research and writing inherent in her academic experience, Lalich also draws upon her eleven-year (1975–1986) commitment to the Democratic Workers Party (DWP). She refers to her DWP experience as having been part of an inner circle of a radical political cult (Lalich, 2004). Part of her unique contribution to understanding abuse and recovery is her combined perspective both as a former member and now from a more objective, academic vantage point.

Lalich has made several significant book contributions (1994 [with primary author Madeleine Tobias], 1995 [with Margaret Singer], 1996, 2004, 2006 [with Madeleine Tobias], and 2018 [with Karla McLaren]) related to religious abuse and recovery. For the purpose of this paper, I examine the past three (2004 and 2006 [with Madeleine Tobias], and 2018 [with Karla McLaren]).

Bounded Choice: True Believers and Charismatic Cults (2004) came as a rewriting of her PhD dissertation and a revision of her first book, co-authored with primary author Madeleine Landau Tobias (1994). The purpose of *Bounded Choice* (2004) was to challenge simplistic conceptualizations of why people join religious or political abusive groups. Lalich desired instead "to advance a theory that explains how normal, intelligent, educated people can give up years of their lives—and sometimes their very lives–to groups and beliefs that from the outside may appear nonsensical or irrational" (p. 1, 2). She referred to her concept of *bounded choice* to explain initial membership, ongoing involvement, and eventual exiting from the group. Unlike her earlier work with Margaret Singer (Singer & Lalich, 1995), Lalich proposed in this book a more comprehensive approach, beyond brainwashing or thought reform. In this approach, she suggested what might be viewed as a dynamic system, to account for relational or religious abuse.

Lalich identified four interlocking structures consisting of social dynamics that can be found in relationally abusive systems. She suggested that these four key constructs act in concert within the group to create a self-sealing system. Those constructs include (a) *charismatic authority*, the emotional bond between the leader and the followers; (b) *a transcendent belief system*, or the imposed worldview of the social system, which eventually becomes internalized; (c) *systems of control*, the overt rules or governing regulations and procedures that determine conduct; and finally, (d) *systems of influence*, the influential, relational group culture that controls thoughts, attitudes, and behavior (Lalich, 2004). After describing her bounded-choice perspective, Lalich provided an illustrative history of and personal research on Heaven's Gate and the DWP. She concluded by crediting her bounded-choice concept as originating from Herbert A. Simon's economic theory of *bounded rationality* (1979). This decision-making theory (2003) suggests that people are in some ways rational and in other ways irrational, depending on their cognitive awareness and social constraints. People make choices, but they are not truly free, with their choices instead determined by a self-sealing comprehensive system.

The co-authored *Take Back your Life: Recovering from Cults and Abusive Relationships* (Lalich & Tobias, 2006) offers an extension and practical application of Lalich's earlier theoretic book (2004). *Take Back Your Life* (2006) combines the sociological acumen of Janja Lalich with the counseling experience of psychotherapist Madeleine Tobias. The result is a four-part book that (a) defines the experience of religious abuse, recruitment, indoctrination/resocialization, and the role of the abusive leader; (b) discusses the process of healing, including a description of leaving an abusive group and rebuilding one's life; (c) identifies the various ways that second-generation family members are uniquely affected; and finally, (d) looks at the various inherent therapeutic challenges one can expect in working with former members of religiously abusive environments. Unlike *Bounded Choice* (2004), this book (2006) includes suggested recovery resources and recommended reading.

Another of Lalich's co-authored books is *Escaping Utopia: Growing Up in a Cult, Getting Out and Starting Over* (Lalich & McLaren, 2018). In this book, Lalich combines her expertise and experiences with those of Karla McLaren, a winning author, social-science researcher, and former member of an abusive New Age group. This book grew from a California State University research project involving sixty-five former members (some of whom were very young and so were born into their groups) from thirty-nine different abusive groups that originated in more than twelve different countries. All of the former members had exited the groups entirely on their own. One valuable and unique feature of this book is that it focuses exclusively on the experiences of second-generation former members, sometimes referred to simply as "adult children of cults" (p. 142). Like Lalich's (2004) and Lalich and Tobias's (2006) earlier books, Lalich and McLaren's *Escaping Utopia* (2018) presents the importance of Lalich's four dimensions of bounded choice: (a) transcendent belief system, (b) charismatic authority, (c) systems of control, and (d) systems of influence (p. 5). The authors then illustrate these necessary elements of bounded choice through the testimonials of the various research subjects.

Religious Dynamic-Systems Perspective

Although Janja Lalich (2004) is the originator of the bounded-choice perspective that offers the more comprehensive, dynamic-systems picture of recovery from religious abuse from primarily a secular vantage point, other writers coming from a religious (Christian) orientation have suggested similar models for understanding religious abuse and recovery in their respective publications: Leo Booth (1991); David Johnson and Jeff VanVonderen (1991); Jeff VanVonderen, Dale Ryan, and Juanita Ryan (2008); Jeff VanVonderen (2010); Stephen Arterburn and Jack Felton (1991); and a relative newcomer, Jack Watts (2011). Unlike Lalich (2004), each of these authors understands religious abuse and recovery from an addictions conceptualization. Among the most-often-cited, clearly representative, and most commonly viewed originators of an addiction-systems approach applied to religious abuse and recovery are David Johnson and Jeff VanVonderen (1991).

David Johnson and Jeff VanVonderen. David Johnson is a much-sought-after speaker, graduate of Bethel Seminary and Trinity Evangelical Divinity School, and in his thirty-ninth year as lead teaching pastor of a five-thousand-plus-member Christian church, the Church of the Open Door, in Minneapolis, Minnesota. He is also the co-author of a helpful book on the Beatitudes (Matt 5:3–12) that suggests biblical themes of grace and love as positive correctives to harmful church experiences (Johnson, D., & Allen, 1998). Johnson co-authored his most significant book, *The Subtle Power of Spiritual Abuse: Recognizing and Escaping Spiritual Manipulation of False Spiritual Authority with the Church* (1991), with Jeff VanVonderen. VanVonderen is a well-known, certified addictions interventionist and previous pastoral counselor (fifteen years at the same church as Johnson); an extended Adjunct Instructor at Bethel College in St. Paul, Minnesota, and a current popular radio and television guest whose work has been featured in several magazines and journals.

Jeff VanVonderen also has been an expert witness in legal cases involving various forms of abuse. His professional life has been rooted in both secular and religious communities. Of his seven published books, several have been translated into various languages and three (1991 [with D. Johnson], 1995, 2010) have focused specifically on religious abuse and recovery.

In *The Subtle Power of Spiritual Abuse* (Johnson D., & VanVonderen, J., 1991), which has persisted through its eighteenth printing, Johnson and VanVonderen have suggested a dynamic-systems perspective of religious abuse and recovery within a Christian worldview. The authors' two-fold stated intent of the book was to communicate the important message of grace and liberation to those wounded by false spiritual beliefs and behaviors, primarily within a Christian context, while simultaneously encouraging the readers to understand that perpetrators of spiritual abuse may also be victims of an abusive system and in need of their own healing (p. 14). The authors wanted to "help both leaders and followers to recognize spiritual *systems* that have become abusive" (p. 25; emphasis added). The authors wanted readers to examine their own religious beliefs and practices. In this book, they have described and defined spiritual abuse (Part I), explaining why it occurs (Part II) and how comprehensive recovery may be achieved (Part III).

Following the book's introduction, the authors have defined spiritual abuse as "the mistreatment of a person who is in need of help, support or greater spiritual empowerment, with the result of weakening, undermining or decreasing that person's spiritual empowerment" (1991, p. 20). Additionally, within Part I (pp. 17–107) they have

- provided a brief history of spiritual abuse as identified in both Old and New Testaments (pp. 29–40), describing some of the false belief systems along with adjoining behaviors (pp. 41–52);
- suggested a predisposition to spiritual abuse based on habituated unhealthy family-of-origin relational patterns (pp. 53–62);
- described the abuse system, including power posturing, performance preoccupation, excessive rules (both spoken and unspoken), and extreme subjectivism (pp. 63–72);
- given reasons behind why people remain in these abusive systems (pp. 73–80); and
- provided examples of Scripture twisting, for the purpose of control and manipulation by abusive leaders (pp. 81–107).

In Part II, Johnson and VanVonderen have described how and why abusive leaders themselves are manipulated and controlled by unhealthy religious systems (1991, pp. 107–80). They concluded that this is due in part due to the leaders

- having a false belief of what constitutes authentic spiritual authority (pp. 107–20);
- accepting pressures to live an unrealistic and inauthentic hypocritical life, filled with double-standards (pp. 121–28);
- supporting the unspoken rules of the church to accept that image is more important than living authentically with the normal struggles of life and leadership (pp. 130–36);

- inverting big and small issues, dismissing individual needs over the agenda of the church system (pp. 139–45);

- giving priority to performance over grace and mercy that can set people free (pp. 146–52); in place of free access to God and His grace, pleasing the leaders becomes more important than pleasing God (pp. 154–61);

- allowing recruiting people to take precedence over simply sharing the good news of God's love and grace (pp. 162–68); and

- operating within the accepted value system within which needs of the leaders take precedence over the needs of the people (pp. 169–78).

Finally, in Part III, Johnson & VanVonderen have offered suggestions about how recovery from spiritual abuse may occur (1991, pp. 181–232). The importance of understanding and avoiding spiritual traps is imperative. These traps entail several imposed messages, all having the outcome of learned powerlessness founded on shame-based relationships as sometimes identified in addictive systems (pp. 181–91). Telling oneself the truth and finding supportive relational reinforcement leads to renewing one's mind from being controlled by unhealthy relational systems (pp. 192–200). Recovering from being extremely self-focused within the spiritually abusive system requires a redirecting of attentions from pleasing the system to accepting the grace and pleasure of God toward oneself, which results in learning to live in a positively transformed way (pp. 202–11). Chapters 20 (pp. 213–21) and 21 (pp. 222–32) include principles and guidance to help one decide either to leave an abusive religious system or to remain and fight the system while accepting the realistic costs. Healthy and unhealthy religious systems are contrasted. In the Epilogue, abusive leaders are encouraged to turn to God's kindness and grace to find rest and the healing that they too need to experience (pp. 233–34).

Similar to that of Lalich (2004), Johnson and VanVonderen's approach to religious abuse and recovery is comprehensive in nature and fits well into a dynamic-systems understanding. Both Lalich (2004) and Johnson and VanVonderen (1991) acknowledged the place and function of the unhealthy, closed/self-sealed system of influence and the necessity of breaking away from it. Unlike many other books on religious abuse, Johnson and VanVonderen made heavy use of a theologically driven framework to understand religious abuse and recovery. Their book also affirms the authentic victimization of the former member, while simultaneously acknowledging the former member's psychosocial needs; the necessity for cognitive reframing on the part of the former member, and all this within a necessarily safe, relational environment in which healing can occur.

These four basic theoretical perspectives—a thought-reform or mind-control understanding; a Conversionist conceptualization; a psychosocial, needs-based perspective; and a dynamic-systems approach—have many overlapping components and values. In varying degree, the authors of each perspective acknowledge the *pervasive problem* of religious abuse; the *inherent challenges* associated with understanding religious abuse and recovery; the *lack of complete neutrality* in their own perspectives; the necessity of having an opinion on the role or impact of *mind control*; and the *complexity and variability of experience* of former religious-abuse members. Finally, all these writers have been *emphatic* in their conceptualizations and *passionate* in making their perspectives known and accepted.

My intention in this chapter has been two-fold: to underscore the relevance of abuse and to identify and organize the four basic theoretical perspectives on religious abuse and recovery by examining significant and representative literature from the past five decades. In the next chapter, I suggest a philosophical/theological standard, or *criteria*, to assist interested parties in evaluating the strengths and weakness of each of the four perspectives.

2

An Evaluative Standard
and Apologetic

IN THE INTRODUCTION OF this paper, I provided six inherent challenges to the field of cultic studies, briefly suggested the importance of the history of religious abuse, identified four theoretical perspectives on religious abuse and recovery, and outlined the trajectory of each chapter to follow. In chapter 1, I offered the historical, existential, and conceptual context to help readers understand the general topic of religious abuse and recovery.

My intent in chapter 2 is to identify (a) an evaluative philosophical/ theological standard, along with (b) an apologetic, or logical reasoned case, which together offer a means by which both professionals and laypersons can assess the strengths and limitations of the four theoretical perspectives of religious or spiritual abuse and recovery previously introduced. Placing both the standard and method in proper perspective, I discuss the unavoidable philosophical and theological presuppositions on which they are based, and the relevance of both for increased understanding of religious or spiritual abuse and recovery.

As I stated at the outset of this paper, everyone has a worldview that represents an interpretive or philosophical starting point that includes an epistemological standard by which each individual understands the world and his respective place in it. One's worldview controls one's thinking, while determining both his understanding of and response to various relationships and life events. Important to the integrity of one's worldview are the need for (a) logical consistency, (b) comprehensive empirical evidence, (c) existential viability, and, in the milieu of religious abuse and recovery, (d) a sufficient philosophical/theological context for understanding these concepts.

One would hope that writing about religious or spiritual abuse and recovery encourages both writer and readers to think about what is propositionally true about life and what is not, and practically, why it matters. However, very few cultic-studies authors present the underlying assumptions that influence their perspectives. Readers are often left to assume that philosophical or theological constructs are either irrelevant or minimally important. In contrast, defining these constructs is both relevant and significant to the topic of this paper. Before I articulate my own philosophical/theological assumptions, however, a brief consideration of the diverse horizon of beliefs reflected in some of the major worldviews may be helpful to readers as a context for the discussion that follows.

Worldviews: A Brief Overview

The largest conceptualizations of worldviews ultimately offer two possible choices: One either believes in a theistic (theocentric, God-centered) world or a nontheistic (anthropocentric, man-centered) world. For reasons that I will discuss in this and ensuing chapters, everyone lives in the tension between these two perspectives. Nobody lives consistently within a stated worldview all the time. For various reasons, individuals may at different times borrow the intellectual and existential capital from views they otherwise oppose.

Within the two broad choices of theocentric or nontheistic are eight distinct philosophical worldviews (Sire, 1976/2009), each identified by its perspective of what is most basic to understanding life (prime reality, or ontology/metaphysics). These eight worldviews, which I describe in more detail in the sections that follow, include

- *Monotheism* (various forms). Reality is viewed as personal and created by a supreme, life-defining being (e.g., Christianity, Judaism, Islam).

- *Deism.* A transcendent and impersonal God is the First Cause who is now wholly uninvolved in the universe, leaving humankind to totally fend for itself.

- *Naturalism.* God does not exist, and the material universe is the singular dimension of reality. There is nothing of a transcendent nature.

- *Nihilism.* Reality is ultimately unknown, and there is no meaning to life.

- *Existentialism.* Reality is defined only by each individual and that individual's life choices.

- *Pantheistic monism.* This view represents a blend of monism (belief in the oneness and unity of reality) and panthesism (the belief that the universe is in some sense divine and should be revered) tells us reality is impersonal, exclusively spiritual, and heavily illusory.

- *New age.* This worldview includes a broad mix of Pantheistic monism while also affirming a positive Western, rather than negative Eastern, evolutionary perspective of human experience that defines all of reality.

- *Postmodernism.* Reality is identified only by the social-environment construct in which one finds oneself, and by the particular self-authenticating language one uses and which is interpreted within one's present and unique social context.

Understanding each of these eight worldviews requires an examination of what historically and logically follows from their ontology, or that which is most basic to each in understanding life. Therefore, a deeper examination of each worldview may be helpful.

Monotheism

A monotheistic worldview suggests that reality is ultimately determined by one distinctive, universal, personal God. The world's prominent examples of monotheism are Christianity, Islam, and in smaller but still exemplar numbers of adherents, Judaism. Each of these religions is broadly similar to the others, yet each differs significantly in its worldview. All three religions affirm that God is an intelligent being, sovereign (all controlling); omnipotent (all powerful); omniscient (all knowing); transcendent (separate from creation); immanent (works within creation); omnipresent (in all places); and holy, just, righteous and creator/designer of the physical cosmos.

Some individuals might point to this list and suggest that these three religions worship the same God. But substantial opposing propositional claims deny this: Christianity and Judaism affirm that God is relationally connective and personal, while Islam asserts that God is autocratic, aloof, and arbitrary (Qur'an 5:40). Unlike the Bible that Christians affirm, in which God is tripersonal (2 Cor 13:14), the Qur'an states God is monopersonal

(Qur'an 4:48); similarly, this proposition is found in the Shema Yisreal, which may be the most well-known definitive statement of Jewish identity: "Hear, O Israel: the Lord our God, the Lord is one" (Deut 6:4). Finally, the New Testament states that the central historic figure, the Jesus of Christianity, is divine (Col 2:9); the Qur'an denies this claim while also denying that Jesus was the son of God (Qur'an 112:2–3); Judaism, as traditionally understood, denies Jesus as the unique personal savior for humankind.

Judaism, Christianity, and Islam differ significantly in the authoritative criteria from which their respective worldviews are derived. For those criteria, Judaism appeals to the Tanakh, the Hebrew Bible, which contains twenty-four books (comparable to the Old Testament in the Christian Bible); the Midrash, a commentary on the Tanakh; the Mishnah, a summary of the religious and civil laws of the Jews, sometimes referred to as the oral law; and the Talmud, a commentary on the Mishnah. The authoritative texts for Islam include the Quran, the most sacred of their texts, and the Hadith, a secondary account of the sayings of Muhammad and his followers. The Christian Bible is the authoritative source for Christians.

Overall, Christianity and Judaism are more similar in their worldview than Islam is to either of them. For instance, Islam views the Christian Bible as seriously flawed. In part, this difference is the result of Christianity having grown more out of Jewish history than from any perceived shared history with Islam (Houssney, 2010). Additionally, an authoritative interpretation regarding the Old Testament is more consistently found in Judaism than affirmed by Islam. Regardless, diversity of belief within Judaism, Islam, and Christianity is substantial, and none of the three is authentically respected if the self-defined and significant propositional differences among them are not clearly acknowledged.

Deism

According to Sire (1976/2009), in deism, "A transcendent God as a First Cause, created the universe, but then left it to run on its own. God is thus not immanent [works within creation], not triune, not fully personal, not sovereign over human affairs, not providential" (p. 51). The external world was created as a mechanical, cause-and-effect, closed system; miracles don't exist, and the world should simply be understood as existing in a normative state, not fallen.

From this worldview, humankind may be considered as having personal attributes, but humans are also reduced to being mere mechanical cogs within the universe. Knowledge is obtained by innate and autonomous reasoning, without divine involvement. Ethics is determined intuitively, or by observation of the external, natural state of being. The purpose of life is to be happy and feel good as determined at creation and discovered through study, evidence, and reason; this view results in the proposition that, given time and natural advancement, the world will inevitably improve.

Naturalism

Naturalism states that the material or physical universe is the only dimension of reality. A comment by Carl Sagan succinctly typifies this worldview: "The Cosmos is all that is or ever was or ever will be" (Sagan, 1980, p. 4). Following this general definition, one might conclude that naturalism does not take seriously the complexity of the universe or of humankind. But naturalism comes in two basic forms. Unlike reductionist naturalists, who attempt to simplify complex ideas, issues, and conditions to the most basic laws of science and physics, nonreductionist naturalists allow for nonmaterial concepts such as consciousness, personal values, and mental states of being.

Similar to deists, naturalists believe the cosmos is a cause-and-effect, closed system not influenced by anything outside of the physical realm. Unlike deists, naturalists view humans as complex machines and believe that any philosophy worth taking seriously should require a "firm [philosophical] foundation of unyielding despair" (Russell, 1957, p. 107). Like the deists, the naturalists believe knowledge comes through innate and autonomous human reason, and they see the world as normative and unfallen. Although some naturalists may affirm claims of personal truth, they deny any ultimate Truth. Their ethics are determined by utilitarian values or by popular preference. If they are consistent with their worldview, naturalists claim no universal meaning to life, but only each individual's subjective meaning, which is exclusively for one's own benefit and will end when one dies.

Nihilism

Nihilism originated in the early nineteenth century and was promoted most vigorously by German philosopher Friedrich Nietzsche (1844–1900). When they consistently hold this worldview, nihilists deny having any philosophical or worldview. In this reality, the external world has no objective order, is ultimately unknown, and is without discernable meaning. Humankind is only the product of genetic mutation, time, and chance, living in an absurd world without intrinsic value. Neither knowledge nor ethical standards are obtainable. At "its core is the denial of objective value of any kind: moral, aesthetic, intellectual and so on" (Groothuis, 2011, p. 342). For understandable reasons, logical consistency within this worldview is existentially impossible.

Existentialism

Existentialism has two forms: *atheistic,* as portrayed by Albert Camus (1913–1960) and Jean-Paul Sartre (1905–1980), or *theistic,* as depicted by Soren Kierkegaard (1813–1855), Karl Barth (1886–1968), and Rudolf Bultmann (1884–1976). Both atheistic and theistic forms begin with a positive core belief in the individual as the only definer of truth and reality.

Humankind is typically seen as capable of using autonomous reason to know itself and the universe. The external world is neither objectively rational nor knowable but defined and transcended by human choices and usually without an overarching purpose. The individual subjective experience of the world is what brings meaning and value. Humans create their own essence. Unsolvable paradoxes are affirmed, and objective truth and moral absolutes are nearly always denied.

Pantheistic Monism

Monism supports the idea that one is all and all is one, and pantheism supports the idea that everything that exists is God. Commonly, pantheistic monism is present within Hinduism, Taoism, various forms of Polytheism, and the Westernized mind sciences (e.g., Religious Science, Christian Science, Unity School of Christianity, and Divine Science), and is sometimes more broadly referred to as affirming New Age perspectives.

In pantheistic monism, ultimate reality and the external world are impersonal, exclusively spiritual, illusory, and generally synonymous with the cosmos. Time is unreal, while good and evil exist only in the mind of the inquirer. By definition, this worldview, in which good and evil are illusory, would exclude the concept of ethics, which exists in the context of good and evil, right and wrong; instead, in pantheistic monism, one finds the meaning to life in one's attempts to blend or join with the universe or with metaphysical Being as a whole.

New Age

New Age beliefs have become a popular Westernized version of pantheistic monism. The differences, however, are significant in that divine humanism is more strongly promoted within a New Age worldview, and the unity of all things typically revolves around the values of ecology and the political promotion of positive cosmic evolution and human potential. Like pantheistic monism, New Age beliefs typically deny the notion of propositional truth, leaving an undetermined standard for ethics, a perspective of moral relativism (found in the Eastern notion of Karma), and a strong, practical belief in human autonomy in all matters. Unlike pantheistic monism, which sees life as forever cyclical, those with a New Age worldview typically prefer to see human aspirations of perfection within a single lifetime as possible.

Postmodernism

From the postmodernist worldview, reality exists only within the context of society and is interpreted through language as a social construct, without fixed or intrinsic meaning or significance. The notion of a metanarrative, such as the stories in traditional religions about how one should live, is dismissed, and claims about absolute truth are typically denied. The very concept of an objective human nature is rejected.

Once again, if postmodernists are consistent with this basic worldview, they affirm on subjective grounds alone that all religions are equally true. Postmodernists gain knowledge and ethical standards only within their unique social context. Typically, their only absolute ethic is tolerance toward others' behaviors and beliefs.

The Standard—A Christian Worldview

As I noted in the Introduction, the philosophical starting point of this paper is within Christian monotheism as generally understood and theologically articulated in the well-known Christian creeds and statements of faith: the Apostles Creed, the Nicene Creed, the Athanasian Creed, or as most comprehensively identified in the Westminster Assembly of Divines' *Confession of Faith* (1647/1976). With the intent of providing a basis from which one can achieve a better understanding of religious abuse and recovery within the comprehensive worldview of Christian monotheism, I suggest focusing on six philosophical questions applicable to any worldview. These questions correspond to six branches or schools of academic study of philosophy. Those branches include

a. *Ontology/metaphysics.* The branch of philosophy dealing with the nature of prime or ultimate reality (as in the various worldviews just presented).

b. *Teleology.* The explanation behind the existence of the external world around us.

c. *Anthropology.* The study of the nature and significance of humankind.

d. *Epistemology.* The study of the theory and basis of knowledge, particularly in reference to its limits and validity.

e. *Ethics.* A theory or system of how we should act toward others; moral values.

f. *Semantics.* How one discerns the meaning of life as expressed through language.

Within these philosophical domains, the six philosophical questions to answer from a Christian monotheistic worldview are

a. How does one define *prime reality*—What is the ultimate reality behind human existence?

b. What is one's teleology—How is one to understand the purpose behind the external world?

c. Of what does one's anthropology consist—How does one view and value humankind?

d. What is one's epistemology—the means by which one finds verifiable beliefs?

e. Once one has identified these beliefs, how should they inform one's *ethics* in the treatment of others? And finally,

f. How does one use semantics in support of one's worldview—or how does one's use of language both assist and reflect one's understanding of ultimate meaning of humankind and of one's own personal life?

The Six Questions, Answered

In addressing each of these questions, which are answered historically and theologically in the Old and New Testaments of the Bible, I articulate in each of the following subsections the relevant standards by which one might examine, understand, and more appropriately value differing perspectives of religious or spiritual abuse from within a Christian worldview. Once I have clearly defined the standard and identified an apologetic methodology, I then apply the resulting evaluative analytic in chapter 3 to determine the strengths and weaknesses of the four perspectives of religious abuse and recovery presented in chapter 1 in the context of this methodology.

Prime Reality

Prime reality is the personal God of the Bible, as revealed in the early history of humankind (Gen 1:27–30): God was directly and personally involved in creating humankind with a purpose, giving them the gift of human relationships (Gen 2:18–25). Following Adam and Eve's sinful choices, God personally held both accountable (Gen 3). And He personally redeemed Adam and Eve through the redemptive work of Christ (John 3:16). Consistent Christians view this proposition of God being personal as embryonic and at the ontological core of the Christian worldview.

This perspective is important to understanding religious or spiritual abuse and recovery because a fundamental flaw in religiously abusive systems is that spiritual abusers persuade their followers to substitute a personal relationship with God with something or someone else as the unquestioned foundation of ultimate personal fulfillment. I believe that until the former member of a religiously abusive environment understands this fundamental difference, one's ability to find recovery and a sense of redemption from religious or spiritual abuse is substantially limited.

Teleology

Having a Christian teleology includes understanding, accepting, and acting upon the truth that humankind and the universe have been created (Gen 2); are morally fallen (Rom. 1:18–32) and in need of loving salvation (John 3:16, 10:10, 15:13; Rom. 5:5–11; Acts 2:14–21), and have an ultimate glorious end (Rev. 21, 22). Such teleological themes—creation, fall, redemption and consummation—define the story of humankind from a Christian worldview.

Religiously abusive groups redefine the purposes of the Creator/God of the Bible. Their false teleology originates from narcissistic leadership, coupled with unhealthy, preconditioned codependency among the members of one's family of origin, and reinforced by the groups' thought-reform efforts. The resulting false teleology identified in religiously abusive groups is in need of correction, as repeatedly identified in the biblical scriptures (1 Kgs 18:17–40; Matt 15:1–20; Luke 11:42).

Anthropology

As noted in the Introduction, a Christian anthropology provides an understanding of oneself and others as having been made in the image of God (or *Imago Dei*, Latin for in the image or likeness of God). Some Christian writers have beneficially suggested that the concept of the *Imago Dei* should be considered an "organizing principle" for understanding authentic forms of Christian spirituality (Macaulay & Barrs, 1978, pp. 13–16). The concept of the *Imago Dei* speaks of the constitution and fundamental value of humans, who are like God in that humans are persons (Gen 1:26).

In contrast to this perspective, religiously abusive groups place little authentic value on its members: their thinking, their natural gifts, and their inherent worth to God or others. The goals of abusive groups, and particularly the leaders, nearly always take priority over the needs of the groups' members. This harmful and negative view of humankind runs in opposition to that expressed in both the Old and New Testaments (Exod 34:6–7; Jer 32:40–41; Ps 145:14–17; Lam 3:31–33; John 3:16; Rom 5:8; Gal 2:20; Eph 2:4–5). The diminished valuing of cognitive development (education, both formally and informally), in abusive groups contradicts the important place of the mind found in both the Old and New Testaments (Isa 26:3; 1 Kgs 3:3–10; Matt 22:37–40; Rom 12:2).

Epistemology

For the Christian, the God of the universe is the source of all knowledge, and His knowledge is propositional in character, which means these statements are aspects of prime reality in the Christian worldview (Gen 3:5; Luke 16:15; 1 Cor 3:20). God has created all other knowers (Gen 1:1; Rev 4:11) and created us to obtain knowledge from Him (Jer 31:34; John 14:7). The biblical view of truth and knowledge contains several distinct components:

> 1. Truth is revealed by God (Rom 2:14–15) . . . 2. Objective truth exists and is knowable (Rom 3:3–4) . . . 3. Christian truth is absolute in nature (1 Cor 8:4–6) . . . 4. Truth is universal (Acts 4:12; Eph 1:21–22) . . . 5. The truth of God is eternally engaging and momentous, not trendy or superficial (James 1:17–18) . . . 6. Truth is exclusive, specific and antithetical (Matt 7:13) . . . 7. Truth Christianly understood [sic] is systematic and unified . . . and finally, 8. Christian truth is an end, not a means to any other end (Groothuis, 2000, pp. 65–81).

Many of these eight distinct components often run contrary to false or distorted notions of truth typically found in abusive religious or spiritual systems. To eventually untangle the false belief system and reconstruct a new and healthier spirituality, it is paramount for former members to eventually redefine the nature of truth and how it is derived. Having a well-informed epistemology, a means by which to identify verifiable beliefs, is necessary because false ideas easily result in negative consequences.

Ethics

For the Christian, the God of all knowledge certainly desires one's knowledge of Him to be lived out in His world. The Christian worldview acknowledges the importance of having a well-informed ethic, driven by justified true beliefs found in both Old and New Testaments and informing all of one's behavior and attitudes. The well-known example of biblical ethics, the Ten Commandments are specifically given twice in the Old Testament (Exod 20:1–17; Deut 5:7–21) and variously reinforced on multiple occasions in the New Testament (Matt 4:10; 1 John 5:21; 1 Tim 6:1; Matt 19:19; 24:20; Rom 13:9). Furthermore, all of the commandments in the Old Testament are helpfully summarized in two, given by Jesus in the New Testament, and the behavioral choices are ideally motivated by the individual's love of God:

> You shall love the Lord your God with all your heart and with all your soul and with all your mind. This is the great and first commandment. And a second is like it: You shall love your neighbor as yourself. On these two commandments depend all the Law and the Prophets. (Matt 22:37–40)

In contrast, religiously abusive systems deny or minimize the ethical benefits derived from the use of one's emotions, mind, or will—in other words, one's entire being. This divine command to be motivated by one's love of God can be a corrective to performance-based spirituality driven by obligation. For the Christian, having love for God originates from the God of love, "for it is God who works in you, both to will and to work for his good pleasure" (Phil 3:12). And God's grace enables Christian ethics, "For it is by grace you have been saved through faith. And this is not your own doing; it is the gift of God, not a result of works, so that no one may boast" (Eph 2:8–9).

Semantics

The message throughout the Old and New Testament is that all of one's understanding of life events is to occur within a larger picture of reality (Job 38:1—40:2; Rom 9). One finds meaning to life generally and personally through one's knowledge of God, even though one may not fully understand at an existential level (Isa 55:8–11). Unlike other worldviews, Christianity originates from a God who provides comfort and love, even within the hardships of pain and suffering. Suffering has a purpose and is not to be counted as a waste (2 Cor 4:16–18). Part of that purpose includes core themes of redemption, reflected in the relational care and love of people who can provide correctives to false notions of God and His purposes (Webster, 1999).

Understandably, many former members of abusive religious systems hate the conception of God as it was imposed by those systems. This reality makes assisting former members with redefining their concept of God (prime reality) and articulating their meaning to life (semantics) both challenging and yet eventually essential to their understanding of and significant recovery from religious abuse. Additionally, a thoughtful and broad-reaching Christian response to the problem of evil (Clark, G. H., 1995, pp. 194–253; Newport, J., 1989, pp. 217–55) can provide former members some level of redemption. Likewise, former members who can employ a specific Christian response to the pain and suffering they have experienced within a religiously abusive system can know both healing and positive growth (Knapp, P., 1998).

Having addressed a Christian worldview framed within these six philosophical areas of study, I now consider what might be the best method, or apologetic approach, by which to compare and contrast various perspectives of religious abuse and recovery. Addressing this question could easily involve an extended discussion of the broad subject of Christian apologetics, but space prohibits my elaborating on the many detailed approaches. Instead, in the following paragraphs I suggest a quadratic approach, a four-fold method to help in determining the value of each of the four basic perspectives of religious abuse and recovery discussed in chapter 1.

The Apologetic—A Reasoned Approach

The method I outline in this section presupposes the standard already outlined and includes particular *dialogical* (person-centered) elements well-suited for an evaluation of religious abuse and recovery. This four-fold approach includes the following:

- *Special revelation*—represents the contextual foundation upon which the other three approaches can be rightfully understood. This approach involves discovering what the Bible directly teaches or infers by principle on particular topics related to religious abuse and recovery.

- *General revelation*—values the world of history, psychosocial science, life experiences, and generally the natural disclosure of the world around us.

- *Emotion affirmation*—acknowledges the existential importance of human emotion and emotive health as a means to determine truth and falsehood, an approach that is strongly affirmed in both the Old and New Testaments (Eliot, 2006).

- *Redemptive profit*—denotes the overall positive benefit derived by the negative experience of religious abuse, not by denying the reality of evil, but by broadening one's view of reality and finding God-generated themes of redemption in the course of recovery (Rom 8:28).

This four-fold apologetic takes seriously the personal need for redemption, exemplified in the hope that nothing, even past pain and suffering, will be wasted; the variability of individual needs, affirming the value of increased emotive awareness; the psychosocial research and findings within the field of cultic studies and related literature; and is shaped and understood within the larger picture of philosophical and theological universal truths as found in the Bible. The proximate intent of this apologetic is for one to better understand religious or spiritual abuse and recovery. As a Christian, I suggest that the ultimate intent of such an apologetic is, to the best of one's ability, to seek to know God and enjoy Him forever (Ps 86; 16:5–11); and with this, to then encourage and support others to do likewise:

> But in your hearts honor Christ the Lord as holy, always being prepared to make a defense [apologetic] to anyone who asks you for a reason for the hope that is in you; yet do it with gentleness and respect, having a good conscience, so that when you are slandered, those who revile your good behavior in Christ may be put to shame. (1 Peter 3:15–16)

My intent in this chapter has been to introduce both a standard and a method of reasoning (apologetic) by which one can respectfully evaluate the strengths and limitations, or weaknesses, of the four general perspectives commonly found in the literature from which to approach religious or spiritual abuse and recovery (presented in chapter 1). Assuming this proposed standard and apologetic method, I then ask four evaluative questions of each perspective:

a. To what degree does the particular approach affirm the Bible's perspective in the six philosophical categories of prime reality, teleology, anthropology, ethics, epistemology and semantics? This worldview question helps to establish the degree to which an approach agrees with the Bible (special revelation).

b. What is the supporting evidence found in history, psychosocial research, and general life experience or the natural world as affirmed or denied from within each of the four perspectives? This question is an attempt to determine the weight of the general revelation reflected in each perspective.

c. What can one identify in each perspective that encourages the emotional health of former members and offers a deeper understanding of religious or spiritual abuse? This question highlights the degree to which the emotional life of a person is valued (emotion affirmation).

d. In the course of developing one's understanding of recovery from religious or spiritual abuse, in what way(s) do each of the four perspectives affirm that substantial and meaningful redemption is obtainable? The answer to this question helps to identify the positive value one may derive from the negative experience of religious abuse and recovery (redemptive profit).

Using these four questions and proposed answers, I will now explore in chapter 3 the strengths and limitations of the four basic perspectives to support an increased understanding of religious or spiritual abuse and recovery.

3

Evaluation of Approaches
to Religious Abuse and Recovery

DEPENDING ON ONE'S WORLDVIEW, various rationale and supporting logic exist for each of the four basic approaches that one might consider for addressing religious abuse and recovery, as I have discussed previously in this dissertation. Now, in chapter 3, I suggest potential answers from each of the four perspectives to the questions I posed at the end of chapter 2, for the purpose of more clearly delineating the theoretical strengths and limitations of each approach in supporting the recovery of those who have experienced religious abuse.

Evaluative Question 1

To review, the first evaluative question I posed in chapter 2 was "To what degree does the particular approach affirm the Bible's perspective in the six philosophical categories of prime reality, teleology, anthropology, ethics, epistemology, and semantics?" As I noted there, this worldview question helps to establish the degree to which an approach may agree with the Bible (special revelation).

Unlike Christian authors, secular writers in cultic studies seldom articulate their worldviews. It is rarer yet that either secular or Christian writers express their worldviews within the philosophical categories of prime reality, teleology, anthropology, ethics, epistemology, and semantics. Therefore, to answer this question, one must both consider explicit statements of beliefs and identify the implied or implicit beliefs associated with the approach, to establish the degree to which a perspective agrees with the biblical worldview. With this disclaimer, I suggest in the subsections that follow how one might evaluate this question from both the secular and Christian point of view, and implicitly within the broader philosophical context.

Question 1: Thought-Reform/Mind-Control Perspective

To review, those who hold a thought-reform/mind-control perspective believe it is primarily the behavioral dynamics of another's undue influence that cause one's involvement in and consequent need for recovery from religious abuse. Culpability is predominantly laid upon the manipulative nature of the abusive group or person(s) in question. Recovery is primarily found through education about mind-control dynamics as applied to the religious environment in question.

The core ontological beliefs within a secular thought-reform perspective are that reality is knowable and may be either personal or impersonal in character (but more often defaults to the impersonal). Lifton himself (although raised a Jew) appears to affirm an existential worldview, as evidenced in his affirmation of Camus (Lifton, 1961/1989, p. xiii), combined with a view of reality that reflects a broad humanist "evolutionary process" (Lifton, 1961/1989, p. 471). In comparison, the Christian thought-reform perspective is that reality is knowable and personal, and has been created and defined by the personal God of the Bible (Martin, P., 1993b). Secular evolutionary beliefs usually include some teleological assumptions, optimistically embracing human development and eschatology; yet they deny the Christian teleological themes—creation, fall, redemption, and consummation, which provide a well-defined holistic story of humankind as identified in the Bible.

In a secular understanding of mind control, human value includes inherent naturalist assumptions that imply a denial of the Christian concept of the *Imago Dei*. A secular thought-reform approach typically derives from evolutionary conjecture relative to human nature and development (Lifton, 1961/1989, p. 471); appeals to recent and ongoing neurological studies about how the brain is involuntarily affected by undue influence (Taylor, 2017); and, finally, draws from autobiographical testimony in defense of mind control (Duncan, 2006; Lindsey, 2014). Ethical standards in secular views of thought reform are psychologically framed and sociologically driven, as originally identified by Lifton (1961/1989). Lifton's ethics are behaviorally defined and assumed to be culturally universal.

In contrast, many Christians affirm the presence of mind-control dynamics, but only as corroborated in principle in biblical text. Christian supporters of thought reform view its ethical foundations as divinely revealed by an all-knowing God, capable of perfectly judging every individual (Deut 32:4; Ps 36:9; Rom 3:23–26). For Christians, the language includes the four uniquely understood concepts of grace, forgiveness, love, and justice as providing four important recovery needs (Knapp, P., 2017, p. 277, footnote). From a secular thought-reform perspective, the concepts of grace, forgiveness, love, and justice are amorphous and psychosocially utilitarian.

Secular concepts of thought reform (Lifton, 1961/1989; Singer & Lalich, 1995; Hassan, 1988/2015) may nominally assume some elements of a Christian worldview, as in the world being knowable, but they marginalize or deny the importance of human origins in offering a sufficient context to define reality. In its avoidance of clear philosophical and theological constructs capable of explaining metaphysical categories, the secular worldview of thought reform typically defaults to naturalism or a vague Deism. Alternatively, the Christian worldview of thought reform is based upon and defended by various injunctions found in the Bible (Martin, P. et al., 1998; see also http://www.icsahome.com/articles/overcoming-the-bondage-revictimization-csj-15–12).

Question 1: Deliberative or Conversionist Conceptualization

Within the Conversionist worldview, thought reform is demoted, and culpability rests with the free and varied choices of individuals. From this perspective, primary responsibility rests with those individuals and the autonomous decisions they made in religiously abusive environments. For secular Conversionists, recovery consists primarily of cognitive education that occurs through the natural developmental process of life experience (e.g., Barker, 1984); for Christian Conversionists, the cognitive education occurs through a revision of one's religious or theological beliefs (e.g., Martin, W., 1965/2003).

Similar to the secular thought-reform perspective, those with a secular Conversionist view assume that reality is knowable; these individuals adhere to some form of naturalism or a polysemic Deism. In contrast, Christian adherents assume reality is created and defined by the personal God of the Bible (Gen 1:1); yet some inconsistently frame their arguments against thought reform using a false understanding of Christian theology that promotes an autonomous freedom of the human will as the ultimate determiner of reality and affirms a false notion of human responsibility (Knapp, P., 2000, pp. 38–41; see also related Theology resources in Appendix C).

Secular anthropological assumptions imply human worth. Rather than using concepts that emphasize theological or philosophical moral failure, secularists typically appeal to religious abuse as a social problem and suggest that the disregard for natural developmental needs of the individual found in questionable religious groups is no different than what occurs in other social settings (Barker, 1984). Some Christian authors affirm a Conversionist perspective, stating, "It's not psychology, it's not sociology, it's not anthropology—it's Christology" (Martin, W., & Hanegraaff, H., 1997, p. 49). In other words, religious abuse occurs exclusively because the perpetrators have chosen flawed beliefs about the nature of Christ.

Ethical standards for a secular Conversionist perspective seem derived from evolutionary values, and typically default again to naturalism. For the Christian, however, ethics are driven by cross-cultural standards of biblical injunctions and empowered by a positive internal passion to follow a personal God (Martin, W., 1965/2003).

Secular adherents affirm the acquisition of knowledge as derived from sociological research and autonomous human experience. Those holding a consistent Christian worldview discover knowledge instead through *special revelation* and *general revelation*, both created and determined by the God of the Bible (Clark, G. H., 1995).

The secular perspectives found in both the thought-reform and the Conversionist approaches exclusively consider psychosocial terms and concepts found in the natural world as sufficient sources from which one can derive meaning to understand and recover from religious abuse. Again, in contrast, the linguistics used in the Christian view of the Conversionist perspective are primarily derived from theological terms and concepts found in the Bible.

Secular concepts of the Conversionist perspective exemplified by Barker (1984, 1995), and the secular thought-reform perspective (Lifton, 1961/1989) evade the importance of the Bible's account of origins as offering a sufficient contextual perspective of reality, once again typically defaulting to a practical Deism or naturalism as their worldview. However, again, some Christians support a Conversionist perspective that appeals to an autonomous freedom of the human will over the sovereignty of the God of the Bible (Passantino, B., & Passantino, G., 1994). Still other Christian writers address this theological error (Knapp, P., 2000; Wright, R. K. M., 1996), appealing to a Reformed view of the human will as found in the Westminster *Confession of Faith* (1647/1976, chapter 9).

Question 1: Psychosocial, Needs-Based Understanding

The psychosocial, needs-based perspective suggests that people join, remain in, and exit religiously abusive environments primarily because of their unmet psychological and relational needs and, at varying levels, people are mutually culpable for their involvement. In this view, individuals' recovery from the abuse consists of meeting their psychosocial needs through education and therapeutic means (typically one or a combination of professional or lay counseling or a variety of support groups).

Similar to thought-reform and Conversionist perspectives, a secular psychosocial, needs-based understanding of religious abuse and recovery assumes that reality is knowable (Langone, 2017a, 2017b; Shaw, 2017; Whitsett, 2017). The consistent secular perspective again typically defaults to a worldview consistent with naturalism or Deism that includes a poly-semic view of God for understanding reality. In contrast, religious (Christian) adherents (Pardon, B., & Pardon, J., 2017) view reality as created and defined by the unequivocal personal God of the Bible and affirm the value of psychosocial concepts and terms for enhanced understanding.

Anthropological assumptions for the contrasting views include that humankind has implied worth (secular) or divinely bestowed worth (Christian). Acknowledgment of moral failure and the need for recovery is common in both Christian and secular perspectives. But the consistent Christian, unlike the secularist, emphasizes the intrinsic and widespread fallenness of humankind, which requires a more inclusive redemption.

Ethical standards for the secularist holding a psychosocial perspective are primarily defined by individuals' internal psychological needs, driven by external social relationships. For Christians, ethics are determined by cross-cultural biblical injunctions and reinforced by psychosocial research (Pardon, B., & Pardon, J., 2017).

Secular adherents affirm knowledge as primarily derived through psychosocial investigation; they minimize or deny epistemological infor-mation found in the Bible. In a consistent Christian worldview, knowledge derives from special revelation (the Bible); but an epistemology that includes natural theology is also accepted.

The secular thought-reform, Conversionist, and psychosocial perspectives all affirm the important role that psychosocial terms and concepts play in the understanding and experience of meaningful recovery of those who have been spiritually abused. In comparison, a Christian understanding of the psychosocial perspective offers linguistic clarity and depth of meaning imbued both with psychological terms and concepts and also integrated within the context of a biblical worldview.

With each secular perspective, a strong marginalization or evasion of the important role of human origins—a fundamental component that offers a broad contextual foundation for understanding reality—exists. The avoidance of relevant philosophical and theological constructs commonly defaults to some practical form of Deism, along with a polysemic theism or naturalist worldview. To their credit, some Christians (Pardon, B., & Pardon, J., 2017) seek a carefully nuanced, integrative approach, thoughtfully affirming both transcendent (supernatural) and natural sources of knowledge.

Question 1: Dynamic-Systems Approach

The dynamic-systems perspective supports the notion that no one influential sphere—imposed/undue influence, deliberated individual choice, or unmet psychological need—plays a necessarily determinative function in religious abuse. Consequently, it is essential for individuals directly affected by such abuse, and those who are providing support and recovery services to them, to recognize and understand the interconnected, dynamic system that religious abuse and recovery encompasses.

Similar to the other three perspectives, those who affirm a dynamic-systems view assume reality is knowable (Lalich, 2004; Johnson & VanVonderen, 1991). They generally adhere to some form of Deism, naturalism, or Christian monotheism in their understanding of reality. Christians who take a dynamic-systems approach assume reality was created and is defined by the personal God of the Bible, and they commonly affirm the practical value of psychosocial concepts, particularly when viewed through the interpretative lens of addictions theory (Arterburn & Felton, 1991; Johnson & VanVonderen, 1991).

Anthropological assumptions of this worldview include the implied worth (secular) or divinely bestowed worth (Christian) of humankind.

Although moral human failure and the need for recovery is readily affirmed in both Christian and secular perspectives, once again the consistent Christian acknowledges the intrinsic and systemic fallenness of humankind that requires a more holistic and biblical redemption.

Ethical standards for the secularist holding the dynamic-systems view may include a myriad of interdependent and determinative factors (e.g., the imposition of a transcendent belief system, charismatic authority, systems of control, and systems of influence) as significant contributors (Lalich, 2004; Lalich & McLaren, 2018). As with the other approaches, Christian ethics from within the dynamic-systems model are ultimately driven by cross-cultural biblical injunctions, but also identified in psychosocial research (Pardon, B. & Pardon, J, 2017).

Those holding a Christian worldview within a psychosocial perspective affirm a dual epistemology as the source of knowledge, including special revelation (the Bible) but also, as in the secular perspective, informed by psychosocial research, particularly as related to family systems or addictions theory (Johnson & VanVonderen, 1991). As with each perspective I have identified, the various terms and linguistic concepts provide significant meaning to individuals' understanding of religious abuse and recovery. However, Christians, unlike secularists, use terms and concepts identified in the Bible to articulate their source of meaning.

Both secular and Christian conceptualizations of dynamic systems are philosophically beneficial in that both avoid simplistic or reductionist notions of religious abuse and recovery. Both secular and religious advocates understand the determinative nature of religious abuse and the broad recovery needs of former members. A secular viewpoint, however, unlike a Christian approach, may easily default to a broad existentialism devoid of a transcendent, holy, personal, and sovereign God as found in the Bible. For Christians who affirm a dynamic-systems perspective, this God has complete control of reality, provides unlimited resources for recovery from religious abuse, and supplies a sufficient philosophical worldview within which to understand religious abuse and recovery.

Evaluative Question 2

To explore the weight of general revelationin support of the various identified perspectives on religious abuse and recovery, I now consider the potential answers by proponents of each perspective to the second apologetic question: "What is the supporting evidence found in history, psychosocial research, and general life experience or the natural world as affirmed or denied from within each of the four perspectives?" The purpose of this question is to determine the existential weight of general revelationas reflected in each perspective.

Since the events of Jonestown and Waco, the body of research has grown exponentially in efforts to understand religious or spiritual abuse and to identify and develop effective approaches to recovery. Although this research is widely acknowledged, significant areas have been woefully neglected. Two of those areas in particular have been identified, including the efficacy of treatment for former members, and research pertaining to the needs of families with loved ones still in abusive groups (Langone, n.d.). There appears to be no empirical research in direct support of or dissent from the four broad perspectives; the influential weight of theoretical research and autobiographical accounts, however, is readily available and may be helpful in identifying strengths and weaknesses of the differing approaches.

Question 2: Thought-Reform/Mind-Control Perspective

The weight of historical evidence in response to the second question from the thought-reform/mind-control perspective derives primarily from the research of Robert J. Lifton and Margaret Thaler Singer, as discussed previously. The influence of both these ideological progenitors is significant to the present-day discussion of cultic studies, a fact easily verified by a review of the bibliographies of cultic-studies literature in both secular and many Christian publications.

Many conceptualizations presented in the literature that are focused on understanding religious abuse cite Lifton, or Singer, or both as significant in shaping (either positively, or negatively) the particular perspectives. Indeed, a portion of the point of view in cultic-studies discussions is often framed as having been informed by Lifton and Singer and their combined theoretical research.

Although sound empirical research into whether mind control is a primary factor in spiritual abuse is lacking, the theoretical research is considerable, although mixed. Recent theoretical cultic-studies-based research, psychosocial investigations, and autobiographic stories of religious abuse yield diverse conclusions. Most evidence strongly affirms the presence of thought reform in religious abuse, although other evidence conveys strong denial, and much conveys a neutral or undecided stance toward the existence or role of thought reform. More specifically, some researchers are strong supporters (Hassan, 1988/2015; Lifton, 1961/1989; Ofshe, 1992; Singer & Lalich, 1995); others likewise are detractors (Barker, 1984, 1995; Bromley & Shupe, 1981; Martin, W., 1965/2003; Passantino, B., & Passantino, G., 1997, pp. 49–78); and still others have mixed views or are undecided (American Psychological Association, 1987; Zablocki & Robbins, 2001).

But what about the evidence of thought reform that exists in the personal testimony of those with direct and substantial experienceof religious abuse? The reported weight of the autobiographical accounts of former members of abusive groups offers evidence to the validity of thought reform (Clark, D., 1998; Duncan, 2006; Hassan, 2015; Lalich, 2004; Lindsey, 2014). Indeed, most of the life-experience accounts I have read or heard strongly support this viewpoint. Yet other autobiographic accounts of religiously abusive experiences deny or minimize the presence of thought reform (Barker, 1984; Doyle et al., 2012; Hutchinson, 1994; Thibodeau & Whiteson, 1999). In thirty-five years of counseling and consulting with those affected by abusive religious groups, I have observed freshly exited former members as typically more supportive of the concept of thought reform than those who have been in recovery longer.

Although the weight of general revelation seems inclined toward supporting the view that thought reform is the key component of much religious abuse, the evidence is in fact mixed; so a neutral stance may be warranted. The diverse or undecided theorists may offer the most honest response to a thought-reform perspective.

Question 2: Deliberative or Conversionist Conceptualization

The theoretical research on behalf of the Conversionist perspective comes from two sources: secular religious studies involving sociological researchers, and Christian/theological countercult apologists. As one would expect, both secular and Christian/theological adherents to the Conversionist views have historically been ideologically aligned based on their philosophical assumptions. However, the sheer volume of theoretical research in support of the Conversionist perspective over time has been significantly offset by a syncretistic shift to a more encompassing position, primarily to the psychosocial perspective (e.g., Goldberg, L. et al., 2017), with an apparent weakening of the deliberative perspective. This change is also evident in the growing research at MeadowHaven (Pardon R., & Pardon, J., 2017), and the significant expansion of ICSA's conferences (see https://www.spiritualabuseresources.com/conferencesevents/spiritual-abuse-conference).

Autobiographic support for the deliberative or Conversionist perspective is sparse compared to that for the thought-reform point of view. But examples for the Conversionist view do exist, as with high-ranking former Mormons turned influential Evangelical Christians (Tanner, J., & Tanner, S., 1989); or a former Christian Fundamentalist turned New Age humanist (Winell, 1993); or a former Catholic first turned Evangelical Christian, and now a resolved atheist (Lobdell, 2009). Each of these stories is an example of the Conversionist perspective.

In summary, some autobiographical accounts, both secular and Christian, and some theoretical research do lend credibility to the position that they support the Conversionist perspective. However, the weight of that evidence is weak compared to that of personal accounts and research that support the thought-reform point of view.

Question 2: Psychosocial, Needs-Based Understanding

In contrast to the current status of the Conversionist perspective, the theoretical research in support of a psychosocial perspective of religious abuse and recovery is both considerable and growing. One reason for the growth in this view may be that most of the formal research and writing on the topic is done by well-established professional clinicians and educators whose source of primary income is more broadly focused (e.g., in their employment as counselors in a general practice, as professors, or through well-established private funding. These conditions offer more time, energy, and resources for research, writing, and public speaking, which may result in more potential influence by these groups than by those representing the other perspectives. The advanced educational background of those doing psychosocial, needs-based research seems as high as, if not higher than, that of others in the cultic-studies field. Consequently, their credentials may engender more credibility to this point of view for those seeking to understand religious or spiritual abuse and recovery. Additionally, the growth of organizations such as ICSA can validate such conclusions. A caveat here is that broad growth, fiscal funding, and popularity do not necessarily equate to legitimacy in conceptual thought.

Autobiographic support for the psychosocial perspective is minimal; but as educational efforts gain ground, this support appears to be increasing. Biographical accounts from a psychosocial view are typically reported by clinicians who are assisting the recovery of those individuals (Henry, R., 2017, pp. 127–34; Pardon, R., & Pardon J., pp. 382–86). A shift toward ecumenical efforts (Langone, 1995, pp. 166–86) and growing professional clinician involvement in religious-abuse recovery efforts also may cause a related shift, from a narrow, thought-reform perspective of how former members view their recovery, to a broader, psychosocial point of view.

Likewise, the weight of natural evidence that supports the psychosocial perspective has been increasing in recent years. This change is evident in the increased number of advanced psychosocial educational programs of "cultic studies in the disciplines of mental health (counseling, social work, pastoral psychology and clinical psychology)" (see http://www.icsahome.com/elibrary/graduate-study). Additionally, the growth of the psychosocial perspective is evidenced in the recent acceptance of certified psychosocial education credits (see http://www.icsahome.com/events/continuing-education/ce-program-policies-and-procedures) for programs that generally support the psychosocial perspective. Finally, growing interest in psychosocially related events for expanding one's understanding of recovery from religious abuse might also indicate a mounting strength within this perspective (see http://www.icsahome.com/events). The evidence from general revelation is particularly strong in support of the psychosocial perspective of spiritual or religious abuse and recovery.

Question 2: Dynamic-Systems Approach

Similar to the increasing support for the psychosocial perspective as a primary means of addressing religious abuse and recovery, the weight of historical research in support of a systems approach to this endeavor is considerable and also growing. A systems approach to the issue can be traced to Austrian biologist Ludwig von Bertalanffy and his contributions to general systems theory (GST). During the 1940s, Bertalanffy reacted against reductionism and attempted to revive the unity of science; he eventually codified his thinking in *General System Theory: Foundations, Development,*

Applications (1968). I elaborate on the significant contributions of Berta-lanffy and others in chapter 4.

Simultaneously, psychosocial research, as identified in *Applying Family Systems Theory to Meditation* (Regina, 2011), reflects the historical advancement of family systems theory that brought a paradigm change in counseling. This advancement has supported a better understanding of religious environments as relational systems (Friedman, 1985). Many concepts and principles found in family systems theory have been applied to religious-abuse recovery efforts (Aguado, 2018; Johnson & VanVonderen, 1991; Knapp, P., 1998, 2000; & Wickliff, 1989). The autobiographical and biographical accounts supportive of a dynamic-systems approach seem sparse (Lalich, 2004; Lalich & McLaren, 2018); I identify potential reasons for that scarcity in chapter 4.

As with the psychosocial perspective, the weight of natural evidence supporting the dynamic-systems approach is expanding. In addition to this thesis, other recent, advanced research projects related to religious formation support a systems perspective (Veenhuizen, 2011; Laymon, 2018). A great deal of empirical and theoretical research in support of this perspective remains to be done.

To summarize the potential responses to evaluative Question 2, the existential weight of evidence (general revelation) varies across the four perspectives. The thought-reform perspective appears strong in autobiographic evidence, but mixed in theoretical research to explain and defend the general view. The deliberative or Conversionist perspective seems weak in most areas of natural evidence, particularly when compared to the other approaches. The psychosocial perspective appears strong based on the theoretical research available, but it is currently weak in providing autobiographic evidence. Finally, the dynamic-systems approach is strong in its integrative efforts to explain and address religious abuse and recovery in an integrated way, but weak in the theoretical, empirical, and autobiographical/biographical evidence that supports this view.

Evaluative Question 3

The next evaluative question shifts from the weight of natural evidence to the importance of human emotion and emotive health in determining truth and falsehood during the process of recovery from religious or spiritual abuse: "What can one identify in each perspective that encourages the emotional health of former members and offers a deeper understanding of religious or spiritual abuse?" This question highlights the degree to which one's emotional life is valued (emotion affirmation).

At various levels, each perspective of religious abuse and recovery acknowledges the importance of the emotional needs of former members. None denies emotions as important to recovery. The difference between perspectives is primarily the degree to which the approach affirms the importance of these emotional needs and the significance of acknowledging and addressing them during the recovery process.

Question 3: Thought-Reform/Mind-Control Model

Consistent thought-reform adherents are most often sociologists who have as their primary focus social behavior, not intrapsychic or emotional needs. Although professionals in this group in general acknowledge emotions as important, behavioral identification and cognitive education are the driving forces behind their understanding of religious abuse and recovery. They typically address emotional manipulation (Singer & Lalich, 1995, pp. 169–72); identify and affirm emotional arousal techniques (Singer & Lalich, 1995, pp. 295, 296), and consider the effects of emotional abuse to the physiological brain to be important (Taylor, 2017, pp. 217–45). However, working directly with emotions is typically secondary to identifying thought-reform dynamics.

All this suggests that professionals working within the thought-reform perspective are more likely to minimize emotions as a necessary means of determining truth and falsehood in the course of recovery. This lack of emotion affirmation as a central aspect to recovery might be seen as a general weakness or limitation of this view, but the Conversionist perspective distances itself even further from emotion.

Question 3: Deliberative or Conversionist Conceptualization

Those who support the Conversionist perspective cite facts related to documented behavior (secular) or beliefs (Christian) as their primary basis for understanding and recovery from religious or spiritual abuse. They consider documented facts to have primacy over concerns about emotional health. On the secular side, an example of this fact-based, educational approach is the independent educational charity founded by Eileen Barker (see http://

www.inform.ac), commonly known as INFORM. On the Christian side, an example is the information-driven Christian Research Institute (CRI), founded by Walter Martin (see http://www.equip.org). Both organizations give little epistemic weight to the emotions of former members of abusive groups. This minimizing of emotion within the Conversionist perspective appears obvious in adherents' avoidance of emotional integration in their determination of truth from falsehood, and it is particularly evident when compared to the strengths of the psychosocial, needs-based approach.

Question 3: Psychosocial, Needs-Based Understanding

It is not surprising that those attesting to a psychosocial perspective typically place great emphasis on the emotional world of former members of religiously abusive groups. Depending on the psychological theory they credit, the value of affirming and working with emotions varies. In the work of John Bowlby (1969, 1972, 1980, 1982) and in other discussions of recovery from religious or spiritual abuse (Henry, R., 2017, pp. 117–38; Stein, 2017), emotions are essential both to defining reality and healing from ill treatment. Others operating within the psychosocial perspective strongly appeal to the role of the dynamics of emotional relationships, and particularly the emotion of love, as being curative (Shaw, 2014, pp. 116–49). Still others focus on emotional trauma, framed as complex posttraumatic stress disorder, as a key factor in approaching individuals' recovery from religious abuse (Herman, 1997, pp. 121). The place of and value in working with the emotions of former members of abuse seem foundational and therefore reflect a particular strength of the psychosocial perspective.

Question 3: Dynamic-Systems Approach

Those who affirm a dynamic-systems approach generally value emotions for determining truth from falsehood in the spiritual-abuse recoveryprocess. But in terms of how they approach that recovery, the importance of emotions is secondary to the *system*, or method, of religious abuse. For example, the secular dynamic-systems approach to healing, framed by Lalich (2004) and discussed in chapter 1 as a "self-sealing" system, or "bounded choice" (Lalich, 2004), says little about focusing on emotions to help a spiritually abused person recover.

Similarly, Johnson and VanVonderen's interpretation of a Christian dynamic-systems approach (Johnson & VanVonderen, 1991) includes little emphasis on the emotional life of former members as an epistemic asset, or means of recovery. Instead, Christians who affirm the dynamic-systems approach tend to focus primarily on a correct theological understanding of God.

A systems approach comprises many interconnected and complex concepts. With that said, the available evidence suggests that emotion, a potential indicator of the truth about the abuse experience, is not the primary focus in the Christian approach to recovery from religious abuse. That limited emphasis may reflect a weakness in this perspective when compared to others. Proponents of each view of religious abuse and recovery have their implied or clearly stated opinions about the important role of emotions in recovery. My research and experience suggest that, of the four, the Conversionist view offers the weakest support for the value of emphasizing emotions in recovery, followed by the thought-reform, and then the dynamic-systems approaches. The psychosocial approach conveys the strongest support for including former members' emotions as a key factor in their recovery from spiritual abuse. In chapter 4, I expand the discussion about the role of emotional focus in the recovery process within a theological context. Meanwhile, there is one more question to consider in evaluating strengths and weakness of each perspective for understanding religious or spiritual abuse and recovery.

The next evaluative question shifts from the weight of natural evidence to the importance of human emotion and emotive health in determining truth and falsehood during the process of recovery from religious or spiritual abuse: "What can one identify in each perspective that encourages the emotional health of former members and offers a deeper understanding of religious or spiritual abuse?" This question highlights the degree to which one's emotional life is valued (emotion affirmation).

At various levels, each perspective of religious abuse and recovery acknowledges the importance of the emotional needs of former members. None denies emotions as important to recovery. The difference between perspectives is primarily the degree to which the approach affirms the importance of these emotional needs and the significance of acknowledging and addressing them during the recovery process.

Evaluation Question 4

The last evaluative question brings focus to the topic of redemption: "In the course of developing one's understanding of recovery from religious or spiritual abuse, in what way(s) do each of the four perspectives affirm that substantial and meaningful redemption is obtainable?" The answer to this question helps to identify the positive value one may derive from the negative experience of religious abuse and recovery (redemptive profit).

In secular viewpoints among each of the four perspectives, the term *recovery* is almost always used; however, the term *redemptive* is seldom used. *Redemption* and *redemptive* may sound too religious or foreign to some, and perhaps overly optimistic to others. For reasons I identify in the next chapter, I use the term *redemption* and the concept of *redemptive profit* as part of the larger concept of recovery, to differentiate the particular (redemption) from the general (recovery).

Question 4: Thought-Reform/Mind-Control Perspective

Driven by naturalist assumptions, the secular thought-reform perspective of recovery from religious abuse acknowledges the importance of recovery, but avoids the concept of redemptive profit. Typically, derived benefits from one's involvement in religious abuse include things such as finding relief from the controlling, abusive environment, with the opportunity to become "much stronger" (Hassan, 1988/2015, p. 278); having the potential to express "emotional resiliency" (Lifton, 1961/1989, p. 472); or experiencing the occasional successful litigation (Singer & Lalich, 1995, pp. 96, 230–35). But, like all secular perspectives, minimal value is placed on the experience of religious abuse as potentially having redemptive value. For the Christian who affirms a thought-reform perspective, the potential exists for recovering former members of spiritual abuse to increase their understanding of the behavioral features of a healthy and unhealthy spiritual life, and to improve their understanding and experience of the Christian gospel (Martin, P., 1993c, p. 217, 219). There is also the potential for increased meaning in their lives through the integration of pain and suffering, resulting in an increased ability to hear God's voice and know Him as never before (Duncan, 2006, pp. 213, 214; Job 42:1–6).

Depending on their various worldviews and underlying assumptions, adherents of the thought-reform perspective can vary broadly in what they identify as benefits of religious abuse. For instance, finding redemptive profit can be a reasonable benefit when framed within a Christian worldview that includes a careful identification of God's means for meeting His redemptive ends (Gen 50:20–21; Rom 8:28).

Question 4: Deliberative or Conversionist Perspective

Coming from a secular viewpoint, those with a Conversionist perspective in general consider one's potential profit from the experience of religious abuse as life experience gained that may be useful in the course of everyday living. As an example, Barker (1984) suggested that benefits from involvement with questionable religious groups may specifically include having the "opportunity to *belong*" and "the opportunity to *do* something that is of value and thus the opportunity to *be* of value" (p. 244). Later, Barker (1995) also noted potential benefits that include having a close comradeship while avoiding loneliness as a positive life experience (p. 127); having the opportunity to discuss religious and other questions not experienced previously (p. 134); and finally, having the opportunity to improve the world in some way not previously experienced (p. 136). These experiences and the learned discipline one has not previously attained may be viewed as benefits from one's involvement in a religiously abusive environment.

A Christian within the Conversionist perspective will primarily suggest that, upon exiting an abusive religious system, one may benefit educationally by realizing the truth of a Christian worldview, and consequently will have an increased ability to discern truth from falsehood in religious and ethical matters (Martin, W., 1977, pp. 355–59). Christians frequently suggest that former members of religious abuse may find a passion for biblical studies and engagement in critical-thinking skills, which in turn results in their having a better understanding and experience of what they view as true spirituality.

As with those who operate within a thought-reform worldview, whether their belief system is secular or Christian, adherents who hold a Conversionist perspective believe those who have experienced spiritual abuse can find benefit from that experience. Both groups affirm the opportunity for education (psychosocial, theological, or both) as the primary benefit one might derive from the experience of religious abuse. However, secularists within this perspective seem more inclined than Christians to support the concept of (redemptive) profit from such an experience.

Question 4: Psychosocial, Needs-Based Understanding

Adherents of a psychosocial perspective primarily frame and understand the concept of redemption or profit from one's experience of religious abuse within the context of the fulfillment of one's psychosocial needs. In both secular and Christian thought, a hope exists that religious trauma does not have to include a lifetime of recovery. From a secular vantage point, some people view individuals' core experience of redemptive profit or recovery as their increased self-awareness and feeling of being less objectified as a result of their past religious abuse (Shaw, 2017, p. 410, 411). Another important secular theme of recovery identified by Whitsett (2017) is that recovering individuals experience a secure therapeutic attachment, which results in the emergence of their "true self" (p. 198). The development of practical life talents, discovering innate abilities or job skills, and experiencing relational growth also have been identified as redemptive or profitable in the course of recovery (Langone, 1995). Within the psychosocial perspective, Christians derive positive benefits by examining the worldview that empowers abuse and from that examination derive a more holistic vision of redemption (Pardon, B., & Pardon, J., 2017, p. 371).

Overall, depending on the underlying worldview of secular or Christian, the potential redemptive profit from one's experience of spiritual abuse is considerable within the psychosocial perspective. For Christians, redemptive profit may also include a recovery process that offers the more inclusive elements, such as a relationship with a loving and personal God, which result in positive changes.

Question 4: Dynamic-Systems Approach

Finally, the dynamic-systems approach to the question of redemptive profit affirms a broad redemptive spectrum. The primary distinction of this approach is that recovery occurs through a larger, more integrated, epistemological lens than with the other three perspectives. Intrinsic to systems theory, and in particular, family systems theory, is the view that redemptive profit occurs through one's understanding and experience of *relational systems*, which are capable of turning "crisis into personal growth" (Friedman, 1985, p. 1).

Both secular and Christian approaches within a dynamic-systems perspective acknowledge the important role of one's worldview (Lalich, 2004, pp. 244–45; Johnson & VanVonderen, 1991). Information is not considered neutral but instead value-laden, rich with meaning, which causes individuals to make choices consistent with their personal makeup and their present environment. Within a secular view, any profit derives primarily from the experience of life integration, growth in resiliency, and the ability to affirm and practice one's personal rights (Lalich & McLaren, 2018, pp. 123–42). Christians operating within a dynamic-systems approach discover a self-image based not on personal performance, but on the grace-filled efforts of a personal and caring God. Redemptive profit occurs primarily in the redefinition of authentic spirituality and experience of relational interdependence one finds in a healthy and well-informed church (Johnson & VanVonderen, 1991, pp. 228–31).

Substantial benefits of a dynamic-systems approach are identifiable in both secular and Christian perspectives. Both groups of adherents consistently affirm religious abuse as not wasted, and both share the belief in the value of understanding abuse from a larger contextual approach than is commonly found in other perspectives. For the Christian, a unique redemptive profit exists that is not present in secular perspectives: the interconnectedness of relational systems that include a personal God as described in the Bible. I define and discuss this unique profit further in chapter 4.

In summary, none of the four perspectives presented in this chapter is comprehensive in view of religious abuse and recovery; but within the limits of its worldview, each perspective has strengths and limitations. With the objective of identifying those advantages and disadvantages, I have applied four evaluative questions relevant to understanding religious or spiritual abuse, to provide a means by which professionals in the field can better understand and thereby construct a more helpful and cogent approach to recovery for those who have experienced abuse in religious environments.

In chapter 4, I offer and advocate for an alternative perspective of religious or spiritual abuse and recovery, SECURE, which I briefly presented in the Introduction. Assuming the philosophical/theological presuppositions identified in the Bible, I will suggest in chapter 4 the greater practical and theoretical cogency of the SECURE approach over the other perspectives of religious or spiritual abuse and recovery discussed to this point.

4

A Fifth Perspective (SECURE)

THE PRECEDING CHAPTERS INCLUDE an identification of some of the greatest challenges to understanding religious abuse, a historic overview of the topic, and a discussion of the core characteristics of four theoretical perspectives. Additionally, they provide the theological and philosophical evaluative analytics that undergird this paper and demonstrate the application of an apologetic, reasoned argument to detect strengths and limitations of each of the four approaches.

In this chapter I introduce, illustrate, and advocate an alternative perspective, SECURE (see Appendix B). The purpose of the SECURE approach is both to avoid the limitations of other perspectives while retaining their strengths, and to provide an improved context for understanding religious abuse and recovery. Following a brief description of SECURE, this chapter has four sections. The first section contains a description of six essential principles of recovery. The second section covers eight core recovery needs and includes suggested reparative activities. The third section offers the framework of seven recovery stages for healing, suggestions for applying the essential principles and addressing core needs, and helpful activities to best determine an individual plan for recovery. Finally, the fourth section includes a summary of the strengths and limitations of other approaches and provides support for SECURE using the same four questions previously applied to the earlier perspectives (see chapter 3).

The SECURE approach has evolved over the past thirty-five years. This evolution reflects

a. my personal experience of religious abuse (1970–1984) in a totalist, aberrant Christian organization (TACO; Knapp, P., 1998);

b. the process of my personal recovery from this abuse through professional counseling and formal education (Knapp, P., 2000), and the mentoring I have received from a combination of theologians, kind and thoughtful professors, a counselor-friend, and others who modeled psychosocial health and mature Christianity;

c. more than thirty-five years of research, writing, and lecturing on this topic;

d. what I have learned from former members and their families for an enhanced understanding of religious abuse and recovery, primarily through conducting life-recovery coaching and facilitating support groups (Knapp, P., 2017); and

e. the remarkable influence of my spouse (Heidi Knapp), part of which was to encourage me to better appreciate the value and place of emotion in the recovery process.

Ultimately, irrespective of the suggested value of one's background, the Bible is clear on the source of any insights I have gained and will yet discover. Consider the humble admonition of the apostle Paul, the author of half of the New Testament, and someone whose *curriculum vitae* included a sevenfold Jewish pedigree (Phil 3:4–6) seldom found in his day:

> Not that I have already obtained this or am already perfect, but I *press on* to make it my own, because Christ Jesus has made me his own. Brothers, I do not consider that I have made it my own. But one thing I do: Forgetting what lies behind and straining toward to what lies ahead, I *press on* toward the goal for the prize of the upward call of God in Christ Jesus. Let those of us who are mature think this way, and if in anything you think otherwise, God will reveal that also to you. (Phil 3:12–16)

This passage and the humility of its author are instructive; irrespective of life experience and education, acknowledging the God of the Bible and His active participation in our lives provides both the source of, and guaranteed growth in, wisdom. As I press on for increased insight about religious abuse, I am cognizant of my dependence upon the Creator for growth in understanding; and I recognize recovery from religious abuse as a concept that for me personally is an ongoing process, not a destination at which I have arrived.

Section 1: SECURE—
Six Basic Principles of Recovery From Religious Abuse

Pressing on is a significant challenge, particularly as one frames recovery from religious abuse as a multilayered, relational *system* that addresses a broad spectrum of problems and possible solutions. I use the acronym SECURE as a mnemonic device to help organize core recovery principles. As noted in chapter 1, SECURE conveys six essential, value-enriched principles to support an understanding of recovery from religious abuse. Simply put, SECURE stands for the importance of the concept and practice of (a) a *Safe Haven,* which derives from attachment theory (Bowlby, 1969; Kirkpatrick, 2005); acknowledgment of (b) the essential role and function of *Emotion,* as found in Emotion Focused Therapy (Johnson, S. M., 2008); (c) the importance of remaining *Cognitively focused,* or mentally attentive, drawing from cognitive behavioral theory (Beck, 2011); (d) *Unconditional positive regard,* coming from the influence of humanistic psychology (Carl Rogers, 1980); (e) the essential benefits in a *Relational* support system, clearly found in the twelve-step plans of recovery (Dinneen, 2013); and finally, (f) affirming the need for *Education* regarding the influences of the family-of-origin (birth family), or applied family systems theory, in a religious environment (Friedman, 1985) as a unifying and relational context. I now consider these six essential principles and their importance to recovery from religious abuse.

Safe Haven

Along with the closely related concept of a *secure base,* the concept of a safe haven originates with the development of attachment theory according to John Bowlby (1969) and Mary Ainsworth (1967). Attachment theory was originally derived from developmental-psychology research into the emotional attachment between mother and infant, which later included love relationships between adults (Johnson, S. M., 2008). Attachment is generally viewed as the significant, long-lasting, emotional bond between people. Emotional bonding begins with an infant's need for an attachment figure (or figures), both as a safe haven in times of distress and as a secure base from which to explore. Research has suggested that children report greater safe-haven support from mothers and greater secure-base support from fathers (Kerns, Matthews, Koehn, Williams, & Siener-Ciesla, 2015).

Considerable attachment research conducted since the early work of Bowlby (1969) and Ainsworth (1967) has concluded that two basic attachment styles exist, *secure* and *insecure*. Maria Boccia (2011), a Christian marriage/family and sex therapist with more than twenty years of biomedical research experience on attachment and the long-term emotional and physiological consequences of early loss, succinctly stressed the importance of healthy attachment when she stated,

> A healthy, secure attachment is associated with a high probability of good, secure friendships and intimate relationships with others in life, as well as lower risk of various mental health difficulties. An insecure attachment on the other hand is associated with a wide range of emotional and behavioral difficulties in both childhood and adulthood. (Boccia, 2011, p. 22)

Early attachment research and the more recent conclusions (Johnson, 2008) have found that human beings rely on attachment objects (i.e., those who provide secure relationships) both for protection and for help to cope with life challenges. As seen within the realm of recovery from religious abuse, this protected space includes a safe relational context or haven, important for one to develop a secure emotional base. This safe haven develops through the experience of emotionally healthy people providing abused individuals with a secure social foundation, or empathetic holding environment, by which they can move forward in recovery.

Boccia (2011) suggests that evidence from considerable attachment research (Kirkpatrick, 2005, pp. 52–74; Miner, 2007, pp. 112–22) indicates that the concept of a secure base is ultimately applicable to those who have been abused viewing God as a safe haven and secure base, and coming from a Christian worldview:

> Attachment to God, then, is not a projection or generalization of human attachments. Rather, it is based on the spiritual ontology of human beings created in the image of God—the unity of mind, body, and spirit given by God in creation, with our capacity for human relationship being an outworking of this unity and these capacities. This relationship with God is primary. (Boccia, 2011, p. 26)

If we view the need for relational attachment from a Christian worldview, it makes sense that a healthy relationship with the God of the Bible is essential for *optimal* recovery from religious abuse. Meanwhile, as creatures made in His image, when we experience safe human relationships, they become *the primary means* of our spiritual formation and psychosocial health, which may lead ultimately to a nourishing relationship with God. While this experience of a safe haven and secure base is foundational for recovery from religious abuse, so is the value of understanding the role of our emotions.

Emotions

Former members who have experienced religious abuse initially present to others in one of two ways: either as fire-breathing dragons, with extreme emotional hypersensitivity, or as icebergs, with frozen, submerged emotions. Neither modes are conducive to recovery; hence, a biblical understanding of the value and role of emotions is essential for emotionally secure relational attachment to occur. Drawing from information gleaned from the Bible, New Testament scholar Matthew Elliott (2006) suggests that a healthy understanding and valuing of emotion includes the following aspects:

> Emotions are not primitive impulses to be controlled or ignored, but cognitive judgements or construals [interpretations] that tell us about ourselves and our world. In this understanding, destructive emotions can be changed, beneficial emotions can be cultivated, and emotions are a crucial part of morality. [A healthy expression of] emotions also help[s] us to: *work efficiently, assist our learning, correct faulty logic* and help us *build relationships with others*. (p. 54; emphasis added)

This understanding of emotion is not found in religiously abusive groups because freedom to express a broad range of emotion is more often treated as a hindrance to the idealized goals of the group. Countering the experience of limited and manipulated emotion found in religiously abusive groups, the Bible clearly promotes the importance of freely expressing a broad range of emotion, as exemplified by the writers of Psalms: loneliness (25:26); love (18:1); sorrow (31:10); contrition (51:17); anger (4:4); pain (69:29); brokenheartedness (147); joy (145); thankfulness (138); praise (95); and confidence (27:3). These varied emotions expressed in the book of Psalms require cognition (i.e., reason, awareness), and both ideally work together as a unified whole to facilitate knowledge. In contrast, religiously abusive groups and some approaches to recovery (particularly the deliberative or Conversionist perspective) seem to devalue the importance and place of emotions.

Initially, former members are emotionally dysregulated; this state is evidenced in their experience of *triggers*. Emotional triggers are dissociative internal or external cues connected to an idea or past experience that result in a disproportionate, nearly uncontrollable negative or a flat affective/avoidant emotive response. Within cultic studies, the experience of triggers is widely acknowledged as a significant deterrent to the recovery process (e.g., Hassan, 2000, pp. 323–25; Singer & Lalich, 1995, pp. 313–14, 325–28; Tobias & Lalich, 1994, pp. 108–14).

Experienced on a broad continuum, triggers resulting from external sensory cues can be visual—seeing certain people, experiencing particular facial expressions, or being in locations where abuse occurred; auditory— hearing certain music or jargon, mantras, ideas, or concepts, or vocal pitch or tone; somatosensatic—being touched a certain way, feeling particularly hot or cold; olfactory—smelling food being prepared, or incense or perfume; and finally, gustatory—tasting a particular flavor associated with a past group. Triggers resulting from internal cues are emotional or physiological in origin; they may include such things as, hunger, anger, loneliness, or fatigue.

Depending on the intensity of the trigger, a resultant state of being, commonly referred to in cultic studies as *floating*, may occur (Hassan, 2015, pp. 279–81). The experience of floating is an emotive, dissociative reaction that substantially hinders recovery.

Recognizing and mindfully countering triggers results in two significant benefits: Emotions can be normalized, correcting the former member's perception of being crazy and producing an experience of a safer environment, which in turn allow for ongoing exploration and recovery. The next section of this chapter provides further discussion about triggers and how their presence may help to determine recovery opportunities.

Emotions are essential indicators of recovery. Decisively working with them both to overcome previous trauma and to help oneself reinterpret reality can determine the depth and breadth of one's healing from religious abuse. Similarly, improving one's cognitive skills and focus provides insights that enable better understanding of past abuse and improves one's discernment for future decision making.

Cognitive Focus

Just as we are emotional beings, so are we thinking beings. The essential role of the mind is commonly undervalued or simply dismissed in religiously abusive groups—the result of two controlling forces, one philosophical/theological, one behavioral. The first cause of poor cognitive skills in this context is that group leaders and members have an insufficient or faulty view of the nature of spiritual experience; they devalue the importance of logic, rationale, and cognitive competence, preferring instead an overly subjective or intuitive avenue to knowledge. The second cause originates in the group efforts to control behavior by protecting the dysfunctional relational system over meeting the authentic needs of the individual. These philosophical/theological values and control of behavior are identifiable within the themes of thought reform (see chapter 1) and are also evident in the habituated values and behaviors that originate in an unhealthy birth family that exhibits injurious rules, roles, and boundaries (discussed later in this section). These two controlling forces—false beliefs and controlling behaviors—devalue the important place of the life of the mind in recovery and so must be addressed.

Former members must be convinced of the value of using their mind to determine true religious beliefs. Then they must learn and practice sound cognitive skills (i.e., reason, logic, and clarity in the understanding and use of terms and concepts) essential to their recovery (see Cognitive Skillsresources in Appendix C). Ideally, combining cognitive and relational health develops into a duel foundation that enables the former members to determine acceptable beliefs and behaviors, a foundation that is non-negotiable if they are to avoid relapse. Without this growth, I have too often seen former members exit one unhealthy group only to enter another, or to return to their original abusive group.

Cognitive behavioral theory is rightly based on the belief that one's thinking, feelings, and behavior are all interconnected. Important for recovery, then, is the need to change one's irrational beliefs (e.g., "I must be perfect" or "The leader is beyond criticism") to more rational beliefs (e.g., "It is okay that I am a work-in-process," or "My past leader was helpful in some respects, but otherwise mistaken or intentionally deceived others"). Religiously abusive groups commonly devalue a rigorous life of the mind, with a preference to simplistic black and white thinking.

Having a worldview derived from the Bible, however, counters devaluing the mind and highlights the important benefits of actively employing it. Consider the many advantages of an engaged mind, as identified in scripture:

- Renewal of our minds provides the means for discerning truth from falsehood (Rom 12:2);

- Cognition assists in naming what is commendable, honorable, and just (Phil 4:4–9);

- Exercising our minds in reflection on God can result in personal peace (Isa 26:3);

- The use of our minds can be a form of worship toward God (Ps 19:14);

- God's use of our minds can be a means of conveying both His requirements of us and revealing the nature of His relationship to us (Heb 10:16);

- The use of our minds can reflect our love of God (Mark 12:30); and finally,

- True and false knowledge about God can be derived by using our minds (2 Cor 10:5).

These affirmations for the biblical value and use of the mind also counter unhealthy dependency while encouraging a healthy autonomy that former members seldom experienced in a religiously abusive group.

It is important for former members of religious abuse to understand why they became involved in the abusive group in the first place, why it took as long as it did to leave, and how recovery may occur. Naming, taming, and then prioritizing emotions and beliefs with language that describes and validates one's thoughts are all essential to recovery. As important as this cognitive principle is, however, people vary in their readiness to address this need. For example, one of my clients had been out of his Colorado communal TACO for more than thirty years before he was ready to use his mind to reexamine his theological beliefs; meanwhile, he had worked hard on his emotional health.

For others, thinking about beliefs may feel safer than focusing on emotions. Recovering former members can often determine the appropriate time to reevaluate a belief system if they are feeling overwhelmed by the implications of either an earlier belief or the revised belief, or simply through using the available educational resources to explore their beliefs.

When former members feel both a sense of safety (a relational safe haven) and have access to resources, the application of this cognitive principle is essential to their process of recovery. To feel relationally secure enough to reexamine their beliefs or explore emotions, they also must experience unconditional positive regard.

Unconditional Positive Regard

Unconditional positive regard is another essential, value-laden principle necessary for recovery from religious abuse. This concept derives from the work of existential humanists and client-centered psychologists following the foundational contributions of Carl Rogers (1956/1980). At the base of this concept are the promotion of unconditional, nonjudgmental acceptance and the positive conviction of a person's ability to find psychological health. When applied to recovery from religious abuse, these fundamental standards can result in an improved religious belief system and practice for former members, who typically are initially self-condemning and often perceive themselves as bizarre or somehow defective among "normal" people without a history of religious abuse. Unconditional positive regard helps establish the safe haven and secure base necessary to enable former members to reframe their experiences of religious abuse and promotes their healthy independence from the imposed spoken and unspoken controls of their past group.

A common denominator across all the perspectives of recovery from religious abuse is the importance of telling one's story without fear of being misunderstood, rejected, or inappropriately judged. Many former members tell their stories of religious abuse and are met with one of three basic responses:

a. *The response is "Well, thank God that is all over,"* as if their exiting from the abusive environment was the only need; this response reflects a denial of the depth of their injury.

b. *They are met with an ignorant, blank stare,* and thoughtful questions are avoided; this response reflects dismissal. Or finally,

c. *The response suggests that only stupid or psychologically defective people join such groups,* which conveys an uninformed, shame-based judgment.

All such responses are hurtful and counterproductive to recovery. Instead, it is essential to offer former members well-informed, unconditional acceptance based on their value of being made in the image of God, and to optimistically encourage them in what they may yet become and yet do with their lives. Following considerable recovery work, this can ultimately result in former members understanding their abuse as not only repaired, or ameliorated by the love of God, but also sovereignly controlled with the divine intent of bringing them personal profit (Gen 50:19–21). More about this view of God's sovereignty is discussed in Section 4 of this chapter.

Viewing unconditional positive regard from a consistent Christian perspective also embodies at least four components not usually found in secular perspectives: (a) a humble and caring invitation for change, originating in the love of God (Isa 49:15; 1 Thess 2:7–12); (b) provision of love that is unique, abundant, patient, and humble (1 Cor 13:4; 1 Thess 5:14); (c) a provision of lavish grace motivated by the matchless love of Christ as seen in His sacrifice for humankind (2 Cor 9:15; Rom 6:23); and finally, (d) the historic context of God's intervention into our world in the person and work of Christ (John 3:16), which provides the motivation behind offering unconditional positive regard to others. But from any worldview, receiving unconditional positive regard requires the presence of healthy relationships.

Relationships

One experiences unconditional positive regard from others only in active relationship with them. Healthy relationships include the experience of a safe haven and secure base, emotional support and validation, encouragement for cognitive growth, and receipt of unconditional positive regard. These combined experiences allow those who have been spiritually abused to reframe, and ultimately to profit from, their experience of abuse.

As a parent of four grown adults and a stepparent of a thirty-five-year-old son with multiple disabilities, I am well aware of how my relationship with each of them provided *roots* (the experience of belonging to a family) and continues to provide *wings* (opportunities for self-differentiation). Healthy relationships include the opportunity for personal maturation and a foundation from which participants can positively influence others. Former members of religiously abusive groups often have a difficult time identifying healthy relationships and are challenged even to have a well-informed view of the concept of *healthy*.

In the support/recovery groups that we facilitate, my spouse (Heidi Knapp) and I model a healthy relationship and help members to define what *healthy* includes. Specifically, we identify behavioral criteria; and depending upon the needs of the particular group, we also may broadly examine the theology behind relationships and, in particular, define *biblical leadership*. The intent of these sessions is to differentiate between healthy and unhealthy relationships, with the distinctions shaped by what it means to be made in the image of God and, more broadly, based on the essential function of psychosocial connections in recovery.

To illustrate, one strength evident in Alcoholic Anonymous (AA) and similar organizations is their emphasis on community and the importance of beneficial peer relationships. I have experienced this directly in attendance at many AA meetings in support of addicted friends and relatives. To encourage and guide the recovering addict to obtain and maintain sobriety, a standard of the recovery process within AA and other similar programs is to have a carefully selected *sponsor*, who is also a recovering addict. Two of my internship experiences were among those addicted to drugs and alcohol. One intern experience was with the Intensive Outpatient Program at the Denver Veterans Administration Medical Center, and the other was amidst those attending the expensive inpatient treatment program at the Center for Dependency, Addiction and Rehabilitation (see Addictions resources in Appendix C). All such programs affirm the essential benefits found through connection with other recovering addicts and with supportive friends and family. I witnessed the incredible profit gained, loneliness countered, encouragement received, and hope derived from the comraderie among fellow addicts and their care providers.

I found that the importance of healthy supportive relationships identified in the AA meetings and both of my internships was consistent. A supportive, healthy, relational community is essential for recovery to occur and to minimize relapse. Similarly, former members of religiously abusive groups must understand and experience the remarkable benefit of healthy relationships because they often feel alone, both in reference to their past abusive experiences and in their recovery. Thankfully, some individuals within the Christian therapeutic and pastoral communities have begun to acknowledge the significant parallels between addictions theory and religious abuse (Arterburn & Felton, 1991; Booth, 1991; Johnson & VanVonderen, 1991; Watts, 2011).

I explore the importance of relationships further in the next section of this chapter when I discuss healing activities associated with the principles of SECURE. Meanwhile, a conceptual context capable of affirming the SECURE approachis needed. To provide that context, I now suggest the educational importance of understanding the basic concepts of family systems theory.

Education

A final core principle that provides a conceptual context for recovery from religious abuse is based in family systems theory as informed by a biblical worldview. But as previously mentioned, everyone seeking recovery from religious abuse has a different readiness to venture into various areas of healing; and the challenges of revisiting one's family-of-origin dynamics can be daunting at best.

A few years ago, a former member of the Branch Davidians at Waco attended one of our support/recovery groups. As we briefly outlined the various recovery topics to be covered in the group, this individual questioned in particular the relevance of various behavioral dynamics and patterns identified in one's family-of-origin (birth family). Specifically, we had suggested that understanding involvement in a religiously abusive environment requires examining the experiences of one's family of origin. To his credit, this participant told us candidly that he was "not willing to go to that portion of Chicago." He meant that, for the moment, he preferred to avoid or minimize this aspect of recovery. For participants to voice a reluctance to address particular areas within the process of recovery from religious abuse is both commonplace and acceptable. The importance of appropriate timing for various areas of healing is clearly supported in scripture:

> For everything there is a season, and a time for every matter under heaven . . . a *time to heal*; a time to break down, and a time to build up; a time to weep, and a time to laugh; a time to mourn, and a time to dance . . . a time to embrace, and a time to refrain from embracing. (Eccl 3: 1–5)

Selecting the appropriate timing for various areas of healing includes that of examining the potential influence of family-of-origin influences in understanding and recovering from religious abuse. In this context, I suggest that core considerations may include the unhealthy experience of habituated rules, and the roles and boundaries former members might identify in their family history that together might reflect a formidable system of influence for their joining, remaining in, and recovering from a religiously abusive environment (Knapp, P., 2000, pp. 96–100).

Family rules, spoken and unspoken, can reinforce the harmful relationship patterns within the birth family. Some of these rules may include

- "Be perfect; be right"in behaviors and attitudes that convey an intolerance of error.

- "Don't question those in authority"; unconditional compliance is the standard of behavior.

- "Don't think or reason on your own"; others will do that for you.

- "Don't feel" beyond a limited range of emotions, and at designated times.

- "Don't trust others," particularly those outside the family (thus promoting the value of relational isolationism).

- "Don't talk about what is wrong in the family; deny conflict; and"— the capstone rule—"just pretend,"idealizing the health of the family.

These unhealthy family dynamics are easily transferable to the experience of similar rules present in unhealthy religious systems.

In addition to the importance of unhealthy, habituated, family-of-origin rules is that of the roles people play within harmful religious systems. These roles fulfill certain natural functions and needs within normal families; but in unhealthy families and abusive religious groups, they are unclear, inflexible, and unfairly allocated. Unhealthy-but-familiar family roles are also easily transferable to roles members play within religiously abusive systems. Within any unhealthy relational system, whether religious or birth family, roles function to preserve the dysfunction of the system at the expense of the individual and result in damage to both.

Additionally, within a religiously abusive system, favorable and unfavorable recognition that members receive from such unhealthy roles is not unlike what occurs in an unhealthy family-of-origin context. The pattern serves as a negative-reinforcement feedback loop that further ensures the survival of the unhealthy relational system. Some of these harmful roles that have been identified in addictions literature (Black, 1981; Bradshaw, J. 1988) and applied to the families of addicts also often exist in harmful religious systems. For brevity, six of the most common roles, which may be assumed by more than one individual, are

- the "addict" (the primary leader in the religiously abusive system, usually a particularly charismatic person);

- the "caretaker" (one who is primarily acting to cover for the unhealthy leader, while also trying to make everyone happy);

- the "hero" (the over-responsible and self-sufficient individual who seeks to create an idealized group appearance);

- the "scapegoat" (one who diverts negative attention from the addict or unhealthy leader, commonly a member who is eventually kicked out of an abusive system, or leaves on her own);

- the "mascot" (typically someone who uses humor or entertainment to lessen the stress caused by the leader); and finally,

- the "lost child" (the quiet, passive one who seeks to fly under the radar of the addict or religiously abusive leader, while yet supporting him).

Coupled with these rules and roles is the important element of the family of origin's approach to personal boundaries. Personal boundaries are "the systems of behavior and/or belief that define who a person is and when not exercised, invites others to determine who that person is or will become. Boundaries, or the lack of them, impact a person's entire life" (Knapp, P., 2000, p. 99). Within religiously abusive systems, four different types of inappropriate boundaries may be identifiable: *the physical*, which reflect who is allowed to touch a person and under what circumstances; *the mental*, which convey the degree of freedom permitted for individual thought and opinion; *the emotional*, which communicate the extent of freedom of emotional expression allowed, along with the level of support for one's separation from others' manipulative emotions; and finally, *the spiritual*, the extent to which allowance is made for the differentiation of God's will as distinct from personal will or that of others. Within a religiously abusive system, as in an unhealthy family of origin, healthy boundaries in these areas are often violated.

In the appropriate time, education about these rules, roles, and boundaries as identified within one's family of origin can help explain a person's experience within a religiously abusive group and identify his recovery needs. As suggested, my thoughts surrounding the importance of these three concepts—rules, roles, and boundaries—originate primarily from the study of addictions theory (Black, 1981; see also Addictions resources in Appendix C).

Some addictions theorists also suggest that a complete and accurate philosophic understanding of addictions would include behavioral, emotional, and spiritual *habituation* (Dunnington, 2011, pp. 67–81). Similarly, I suggest that unresolved habituation of harmful family-of-origin values, with the resulting behaviors of damaging rules, unhealthy rigid roles, and inadequate personal boundaries, significantly predisposes one for membership in a religiously abusive group. I have found that understanding religious abuse and recovery through a family-systems model offers healing from the abuse individuals have experienced both in dysfunctional families of origin and from unhealthy religious groups. Finally, in connecting these two relational systems, I am not suggesting a linear causation, but only a correlation.

Countering one's habituated relational dynamics of rules, roles, and boundaries helps to ensure healthier future religious or spiritual choices for the individual. I explore this view further in the next section of this chapter. Additionally, I identify eight core recovery needs and suggest healing activities that have been helpful to my own recovery and have been identified similarly by others in their recovery experience.

Section 2: ASCRIBED—
Eight Core Recovery Needs and Associated Healing Activities

Following religious abuse, former members often feel overwhelmed by the challenges before them and confused about what to think and do for their recovery. Feeling emotionally flooded and intellectually perplexed is commonplace both for those seeking recovery and those who are supporting them in their healing journey. Before former members and their support team can help shape an individualized plan of recovery, it is important for the team to clearly identify and help the former members organize the various recovery needs.

In this section, I introduce the acronym *ASCRIBED* as a mnemonic device to briefly identify eight core recovery needs. I also suggest related healing activities, many of which inevitably overlap in meeting various needs. *ASCRIBED* refers to the importance of engaging in *Altruistic* activity to provide unselfish support for others; becoming more *Self-differentiated*, able to distinguish thoughts from feelings (both one's own, and separating one's own from those of others); correcting *Cognitive acedia*, to alter a slothful or uninformed attitude about the life of the mind; restructuring one's *Relational world*, to replace unhealthy relationships with healthy ones; redefining one's *Identity* by entering a journey of self-discovery to better understand and appreciate oneself; growing in recognition of true and false *Beliefs,* reexamining claims of religious truth while also acknowledging the importance of primary and secondary beliefs; reducing *Emotional dysregulation*, which entails contending with the presence of emotional triggers that easily prevent ongoing recovery; and finally, addressing the *Daily practical needs of life*, such as personal health, housing, appearance/hygiene, employment, and fiscal assets. I now consider these eight core needs and suggest recovery activities associated with them.

Altruism

One primary reason many individuals become involved in religiously abusive groups is those groups' apparent selfless concern for others. Then, once they are out of an abusive group, former members often continue in their interest to help others. When they have experienced little recovery from their abusive experiences, their expression of this core need may result in attempts to *fix others* who may have harmed them, or to *rescue* remaining members of the abusive group. However, seldom does either of these early efforts produce positive outcomes. In contrast, productive attempts at altruism can encourage a positive sense of self that results in a desire to know oneself better.

Broadly speaking, for former members to meet this need for altruism requires that they (a) have the experience of being heard and validated within a safe environment, (b) reframe their victimization in a process that includes beneficial life education, and finally (c) discover the personal profit, or benefit, they can realize from the experience of religious abuse, to counter the sense of lost time, depleted fiscal resources, and broken relationships they have experienced. To be heard and validated, many former members find a safe haven and secure base within support/recovery groups designed for those who have experienced religious abuse. Because religious abuse occurs in diverse groups, all of which embody various thought-reform behaviors (see chapter 1), support can come from a broader range of former members than just the particular group the former members left. When support/recovery groups specifically for those who have experienced religious abuse are not available, groups focused on codependency, addiction, or trauma issues can be beneficial. A variety of recovery groups focused on religious abuse are also available for consideration on the Internet. Support groups offer much in terms of recovery, and these other group experiences can be altruistically beneficial, both for former members and for others.

Many former members become involved in secular or Christian organizations that provide education and support to those in recovery from spiritual abuse. Participation in these organizations can help meet the core recovery need to help others. For example, the International Cultic Studies Association (ICSA) is largely secular and, like its Christian counterpart (i.e., Christian Research Institute [CRI]), seeks to support, educate, and encourage former members (see related Cultic Studies Organizations resources in Appendix C). Former members can find a variety of opportunities within these organizations—writing articles or books, speaking at conferences, assisting in administrative details, providing lay or professional counseling, and contributing art projects, all of which can help them process their own emotions and at the same time assist others in recovery. Depending on their degree of recovery, area of interest, expertise, and history, the choice of things former members can do within these organizations is broad and growing.

For former members of spiritual abuse who are still too easily triggered by religious discussion of any sort, other options are available. Examples of options that can help former members meet this altruistic need include volunteering in secular environments such as food banks, pet shelters, assisted living centers for the handicapped or senior communities; or being on a governing board of a nonprofit organization. For others, a more personal approach, such as owning and caring for a pet, may be helpful. Getting a dog may be a particularly good choice because dogs typically offer unconditional acceptance and approval not often found with other animals.

Self-Differentiation

Self-differentiation is one's ability to identify the difference between one's own feelings and thoughts, and also to separate others' thoughts and feelings from one's own. Unhealthy religious systems devalue the individual personality: An individual is not permitted to be himself and ends up living another's goals and ambitions. In abusive groups, the individual's identity disappears, and this lack of self-differentiation results in group-think, a psychosocial phenomenon whose purpose is to bring group harmony and conformity at all costs.

The experience of participating in an abusive group doesn't occur out of nowhere, without prior personal history. I contend that very few people join an abusive religious system without previous familial influence that has contributed to low levels of self-differentiation. I have often identified this family-history correlation in working with former members. In recovery work, whether as a former member or in a supportive role, it is helpful to explore one's emotional experience within one's birth family to identify patterns of behavior and find ways to promote improved self-differentiation if that seems appropriate. A family-systems therapist also can provide education and support for gaining a better understanding of one's familial history. Part of this exploration of family history may entail constructing a *genogram*, an historical pictorial display of family relationships, to increase insight about the presence of multigenerational patterns(Galindo, Boomer, & Reagan, 2006).

Exploring family-of-origin contributions in the course of recovery, however, often feels threatening, both to former members and to their families. A stepping-stone alternative might be educating oneself about thought-reform (Lifton, 1961/1989) and its role within a particular abusive religious system, which can lend support to improving self-differentiation. Consulting with a thought-reform consultant may help an individual to identify the negative contributions of an abusive group (see Thought Reform Consultants resources in Appendix C). Meeting the core need for improved self-differentiation is a process that requires time, education, and well-informed resources, including individuals who are familiar with the thought-reform process and family-systems theory. Finally, to benefit from this information requires cognition.

Cognitive Acedia

In the context of spiritual abuse, *cognitive acedia* refers to one's profound indifference to using, or inability to properly use, cognition (mental action or process) to acquire the knowledge necessary to accurately interpret reality. Rather than support the normal process of cognitive development, abusive religious systems encourage a child-like dependency of members upon leadership. In such systems, the acedia, or laziness in mental efforts, is compounded by the presence of thought-reform dynamics. The interdependent and interactive techniques of thought reform inhibit independent cognition and easily result in the abusive control of leadership. However, recovery from cognitive acedia is possible.

Countering cognitive acedia may start with cultivating *hypomone* (Greek term for "patient endurance," used in Heb 10:32; Rom 5:3–5) to stabilize the functioning of one's will, thus allowing for cognitive growth. As an example, the constancy one finds in a routine occupation or other mundane repetitive activity can shape a tenacious attitude and a focused awareness. When the will is stabilized, it is easier to train the mind to think more clearly and effectively.

Initially, former members may not be interested in formal education, but they can still exercise their mind in a variety of ways. They can read about religious abuse that may spark their interest to further their knowledge on the topic, while improving their ability to think more objectively. Comparing biographic and autobiographic stories of religious abuse can bring cognitive clarity to one's own experience (see Redemptive Stories resources in Appendix C). Reading well-written books of any sort encourages one toward sound thinking and energized cognitive processing. Additionally, writing about one's personal experiences of religious abuse, or writing about most anything, can help one process buried emotions, improve cognitive clarity, and expand one's thoughts about life in general.

Finally, a host of other activities help produce increased brain function: having a proper diet, exercising regularly, experiencing a change of scenery, belonging to a book club, or mindfully jotting down ideas or notes for further processing. Developing friendships with people who express themselves clearly can encourage former members to be more articulate and thus contribute to their improved cognition skills. Other people are broadly influential on former members, not only in developing their cognitive world, but also for helping to meet their recovery needs in a host of ways.

Relational World

The greatest core recovery need of those who have been religiously abused is to gain insight about and experience with healthy relationships. An adjunct aspect of this need is being able to let go of unhealthy relationships. Meeting this complex recovery need is the most difficult and, when one is successful, also the most rewarding—a correspondence that is not surprising. In the course of thirty-five years of working with those who have been religiously abused, I have found that many of them have come from relationally unhealthy birth families. There is often a familial history of damaging rules; unhealthy, rigid roles; and inadequate personal boundaries. These individuals carry this habituated history with them into the unhealthy religious group, where the familiar rules, roles, and boundaries are again reinforced and empowered with a transcendent authority. Former members need recovery both from the negative experiences of their family of origin and from the damaging influence of the religious group that may have acted like and promoted itself as an alternative family.

Former members can meet this core relational need in a variety of ways. As previously mentioned, one such resource is participation in a well-run support group, which can provide hope and positive, life-affirming outcomes through the practice that a healthy group dynamic models and offers (see Support Group resources in Appendix C). Within support groups, former members are free to question their past relationships, experience new ones, and acquire an improved vision for future group experiences. And while such supportive groups are significant, so too is experience with healthy individuals, which may come in the form of mentors, life-recovery coaches, and various professional clinicians, in addition to nonprofessional counselors or well-informed clergy.

Spouses who have experienced religious abuse jointly with their mate have the potential to be the most significant positive or negative support in recovery. When the unhealthy role of a domineering husband, an overly submissive wife, or both were present in a former group, relational resources specific to redefining marital roles are helpful. One such resource is Christians for Biblical Equality (https://www.cbeinternational.org; see also the related Marriage resources in Appendix C). Many former members have attested to the educational benefits they derived from this organization, including the experience of attending the marriage conferences it offers. Additionally, general education about rules, roles, and boundaries as specifically applied to marriage (Cloud & Townsend, 2008) can develop one's thoughts about healthy and unhealthy relationships more broadly. In active efforts to redefine their relational world, former members inevitably become aware of new individual identities that support self-differentiation. Former members were not encouraged to think or feel as unique persons, which hindered their intrapsychic sense of self. To recover and grow their own self-images requires meeting another essential need—healthy personal identities.

Identity

For the former member, discovering one's identity is a journey of self-discovery to better understand and appreciate who one is, and who one is not. This process begins *in utero*, proceeds through the influence of one's birth family, becomes stifled when one joins an abusive religious group, and then, as an essential need for recovery, requires renewal and growth. In working with former members, I often hear stories of how their God-given identity has been reshaped in the image of others, rather than conveying them as individual image-bearers of a loving God (Gen 1:27). As a Christian, I believe we were lovingly crafted by God in the womb, and that in knowing this we can find great joy (Ps 139:13–16). For former members, coming to this conclusion takes time and processing, and it may occur through a variety of means. Having worked with my identity formation and assisting others with theirs, I recognize the benefit of exploring one's past history, being honest about one's present reality, and finally, identifying future, long-term life goals or dreams. Former members benefit from exploring these time-specific contributors to their unique identities.

To understand the past requires individuals to carefully reconsider both their familial and religious abuse histories. Accomplishing these steps may include working with a grief counselor to carefully process various losses. Reconnecting with loved ones or close friends could help them identify historic passions and talents from their past. Revisiting old school annuals, family photo books, and home videos, or attending school reunions all can lead to rediscovered interests and natural gifting that may have been pushed aside. Exploring the past can be hard work, but it helps answer how religious abuse kept former members from psychological, social, and occupational development, all of which shape personal identity. Understanding the past allows for and supports improved life functioning in the present.

We are all emotional beings from birth, and then are further defined by the things we choose to do. Involvement in a religiously abusive group seldom includes fun activities that support a deeply enjoyed life. In the abusive system, spirituality is performance based, not grace based. By this I mean that within the abusive group nothing comes free; every benefit gained has a price, and the price is not cheap. Receiving unconditional acceptance is replaced with receiving obligatory work that excludes the experience of fun for fun's sake. For healing, former members benefit by participating in newfound or reexperienced recreational activities, communing with nature, enjoying a previously forbidden food or experience,

practicing solitude, and perhaps taking a much-needed vacation. Such activities contribute to renewed emotions and energize former members to
explore more of life, and of who they are in that life. In the process of identity formation, speculating about or dreaming of what their future might
holdcan also be very helpful.

A *bucket list* is a list of things we want to do before we "kick the bucket,"
or die. Writing down a bucket list can be an exercise in building one's hope
and life vision for the future and, in turn, can lead to a self-determined
identity that culminates in a legacy. To shape an ongoing bucket list, reading or watching movies about others with immense challenges before them
can be inspirational and motivate one to develop and to initiate personal
goals. Think of such people as William Wilberforce, who had a life goal
of abolishing the slave trade in England; Martin Luther, who brought significant positive changes to the Christian church; or anyone with severe
physical or mental disabilities who has persevered and done so with great
success. Whether they involve exploring the past, being engaged in the
present, or writing about future dreams, all these options can contribute to
reshaping the identity of former members.

Beliefs

Basic beliefs typically present in religiously abusive groups encourage
manipulation to more easily occur and can often be predictive of eventual
exploitation. As a former member and having worked with many abused
members from various groups, I have found two false and controlling beliefs that are nearly always present in abusive groups and must change for
recovery. One belief focuses on who or what has ultimate spiritual (Truth-
defining) authority within the group. The second belief or mindset reflects
limitations in the objectivity present when one is attempting to identify
authentic spiritual experiences. A number of helpful activities support improved acumen to contend with such beliefs and enable former members
to distinguish more broadly and clearly among many false and true beliefs.

In this context, some former members may find seminary or formal
philosophical training beneficial, but others can acquire improved discernment through a host of other activities. Temporarily borrowing from another's already-well-developed ability to distinguish true from false claims
can help former members who are struggling with this challenge. By this
I mean that developing a relationship with a theological or philosophic

?h, or another well-informed person can be a stepping stone
l learning. Reading historic theological or philosophical
vide a good foundation for learning to distinguish true from
/hen the Bible is used in defense of a belief, learning com-
standards of biblical interpretation (the historic principles of
hermeneutics) can be beneficial (see Hermeneutics resources in Appendix
C). The study of philosophical apologetics, or methods of reasoning to determine truth from falsehood, can increase one's cognitive ability to evaluate belief systems for strengths and weaknesses, such resources abound
(see Apologetics resources inAppendix C). If their emotional triggers can
be sufficiently contained, former members might visit various churches or
spiritual institutions to compare beliefs, as long as they do so with a safe,
mature, and well-educated friend. Following such visits, processing the
experiences with this friend can clarify the belief systems of others and
remove the ambiguity in the former members' own beliefs.

Abusive groups typically deny the existence of primary and secondary
beliefs. The black-and-white thinking of such groups produces little tolerance for difference of opinion in the belief system. The phrase *one size fits
all* applied to beliefs seems to be a predictor of eventual abuse. Members
of a healthy church or religious institution hold both essential and nonessential beliefs, and there is loving toleration for people who hold differences
in the nonessentials. Even in the essentials, a nourishing church or religious
organization shows authentic compassion and care for those who disagree.
This approach is not the norm in an abusive religious system. Depending
on the type and level of abuse they have experienced, it takes time before
those who have been religiously abused can attend, and perhaps eventually
join, a healthy church. Should a healthy church involvement become the
experience of the former member of religious abuse, then the church may
support the individual's need to define true from false beliefs while also
learning about essential and nonessential views.

Emotional Dysregulation

Following religious abuse, emotions are commonly scattered and need
stabilization to become a recovery asset rather than a liability. One of the
most significant challenges to early recovery from religious abuse is the
struggle for emotional regulation. Emotional dysregulation is typically
identified by the presence of triggers. Without becoming mindfully aware

of and successfully countering these triggers, former members make little progress in their recovery. The most prevalent initial emotions are anger, confusion, depression, and disillusionment. These negative emotions are energy draining, and for recovery to occur, the positive emotions of hope, encouragement, joy, pleasure, and peace must become dominant. Success in emotional regulation requires activities that build *routines*, *repeat* positive experiences, develop healthy *relationships*, and finally, cause *recall* of success (the four Rs). Experiencing the four Rs helps stabilize emotions, reduce triggers, and support emotional growth.

A variety of specific activities contribute to emotional stability and can reduce the negative influence of triggers. In our culture and time, when people think of resolving emotional dysregulation, the first thing that comes to mind is professional counseling. Depending on the depth of damage, professional counseling, and the counseling modality of emotion-focused therapy (EFT) in particular, can help(see related Attachment/EFT resources in Appendix C). This form of therapy directly focuses on emotions and their important role in repairing past trauma and developing healthy relationships. Likewise, artistic endeavors may contribute to this essential need to heal emotional dysregulation. Many former members find emotional release through participating in things such as music, painting, drama, dance, poetry, or sculpturing. These activities can help former members expose and process buried pain and suffering, thus leading to further recovery. Such artistic endeavors can provide energy, emotional support, and encouragement. Attending a comedy club or some other source of humor can energize emotions in a positive way. Developing the discipline to write in incremental stages about one's emotional experiences in an abusive environment also can disempower negative emotions and improve beneficial cognitive reflection. And as already discussed, becoming involved in safe and secure support groups can provide emotive stability, and also meet many other essential needs, thus countering emotional dysregulation. And finally, to complete this brief overview of the eight core recovery needs symbolized by *ASCRIBED*, it is also important for recovering members to address their daily physical and practical needs.

Daily Needs

Often, religiously abusive systems promote unhealthy dependence in members when it comes to meeting the basic requirements of day-to-day living.

Consequently, many former members leave their abusive religious system unprepared for life outside their group and have limited knowledge about how to meet their daily needs.

Daily needs encompass things such as recovery and maintenance of one's personal health, safe and secure housing, basic appearance/hygiene, meaningful employment, and finally, sufficient fiscal assets. Former members often struggle with these practical recovery issues, which require time and attention, and often involve multiple resources. As with former members' psychosocial developmental needs, there also are specific recovery activities that can help them meet the physical and practical necessities of daily life. Getting such practical recovery needs met is humbling and requires both creativity and flexibility.

Former members can recover and maintain their health by joining an inexpensive recreation center or, if affordable, with the support of a personal trainer. Medical doctors and dentists often will contribute health advice and suggest other beneficial resources. A visit to a foodbank may improve dietary options to better meet basic requirements. If these relationships remain intact, friends or relatives sometimes also can be sources of support or assistance to help former members meet housing needs. Social-service resources, local YMCAs, or large, well-funded churches may also provide lodging options. Additionally, some former members find much-needed temporary housing by managing apartments or a storage facility. Often, former members can meet their need for an improved physical appearance by a visit to a Goodwill or other thrift store, and with the aid of an inexpensive barber or beautician-training-school discount option. An honest and caring friend or relative may also offer helpful coaching in matters of hygiene that may support attaining employment.

Similar to someone who has been in the military, for instance, some former members also develop skills and experience within unhealthy religious systems that may translate to occupations outside their former group. They sometimes develop various disciplines and a strong work ethic while in the abusive groups that may become an employment asset. These former members may creatively draw from their background and brainstorm with a skilled occupational counselor to identify employment that will best meet this need. Finally, it is important to build sustainable fiscal assets to help sustain the other daily needs. A financial planner, or well-inform friend or relative may provide assistance in this fiscal struggle.

The numerous and diverse needs of former members of a religiously abusive group can easily feel overwhelming to all involved. In this section, I have sought to clearly identify and organize eight core recovery needs and suggest helpful activities to benefit both former members and their supporters. In the next section, I identify seven recovery stages that comprise the process of healing. These distinctive stages bring together the essential recovery principles and many varied needs discussed to this point and offer further insight into the potential pace and scope of healing activities that represent an individual plan of recovery.

Section 3: A Seven-Stage Process of Recovery

I now identify and briefly discuss seven distinct stages in recovery from spiritual abuse. These stages affirm the many and varied recovery needs presented in the previous section and are useful in prioritizing activities and determining individual recovery plans.

Former members of abusive groups are unique individuals, with distinctive histories that each person experiences in a particular way. Consequently, it is no wonder that what works for one former member may not meet the needs of another. At the same time, I suggest that a basic recovery process exists which, when used as part of the foundation for providing support for recovery from religious abuse, helps normalize the experience of former members and offers them and their supporters understanding and hope. I suggest that a program model for optimal recovery from religious abuse is one that incorporates and supports the following stages of recovery:

- Stage 1—Lacking awareness of one's needs
- Stage 2—Experiencing emotional or cognitive snapping, or both
- Stage 3—Showing unproductive, heightened behavioral activity
- Stage 4—Struggling to identify a relational-based recovery team
- Stage 5—Exploring and discovering life outside the past abusive group
- Stage 6—Preserving self-recovery; struggling with excessive support to others
- Stage 7—Providing a consistent, well-informed, empathic holding environment for other former members

Each stage builds upon the contributions from other stages and creates an interconnected system of influence for successful recovery. Stages 1, 2, and 7 are fixed, the other stages are interchangeable in terms of the order in which they might occur, but they usually follow this general pattern. I briefly describe these seven stages in the following subsections.

Stage 1

The initial stage of recovery takes place while members are still in the abusive religious group. Oblivious to their need for healing, the current members *lack awareness* of their future recovery-support system already taking shape. Evidence of this upcoming support system may come as attempts for relational attachment or emotionally driven invitations to connect with each other for mutual benefit (Johnson, S., 2019, pp. 6–10). Such efforts for attachment may comedirectly from a relative or past friend; attempts by former members to connect with the current ones; or a host of other combining factors that eventually result in current members leaving, which thereby alters their relationships. Often, this process is also coupled with current members experiencing a vague sense that their needs are not being met within the group as they had hoped.

During this stage, the altruistic group efforts are meeting the interests and needs of the group as a whole while denying the individual needs of members. Members are not self-differentiated and are unknowingly insecure in this fact. They have neither a safe haven nor a secure base. Their emotions are highly manipulated by the unhealthy functioning of the group members, and particularly by the group's leadership. Similarly, cognitive functioning is controlled by the leaders, and cognitive acedia reigns. Members' need to experience unconditional positive regard is denied. The relational world of the members is a coordinated, closed system, with rigid external boundaries for nonmembers and nonexistent or unhealthy permeable boundaries for those within the group. The members' identities have been defined by group needs, and individual efforts for independent identity formation are dismissed or highly restricted. Nearly all the group-held beliefs are black and white in character, determined by poorly informed leadership, and often without formal theological or philosophical training, particularly at the graduate level. Current members have no awareness of, nor interest in, making the connection between their earlier, habituated family dynamics and the current functioning of their group.

Stage 2

The second stage of recovery often begins with the experience of an *emotional or cognitive snapping response* in current members caused by a deep disappointment, disillusionment, pain, exhaustion, or suffering within the group. Their sense of having had a safe haven or secure base within the abusive group is dissolving and causing them emotional disequilibrium. The adventure of self-differentiation is just beginning. Cognitive acedia is obvious, but a flicker of change is growing. Soon-to-be former members become vaguely aware of the lack of unconditional acceptance, but this awareness grows quickly. Their relational world is in flux, as is their identity as members. They still have no knowledge of the role of birth-family dynamics and no understanding of how the abusive religious system truly works. The beliefs of the group are typically still in place, but they are gradually being challenged as members' awareness increases. Their immediate physical needs of daily life may delay their exit, but the process that has begun, inevitably brings them out of the group.

Stage 3

The third stage in the process of recovery occurs immediately upon members' exit from their group. It is characterized by *heightened behavioral activity*, typically in the form of uninformed, unproductive, and naïve altruism. Former members desperately want to *do something* to counter the influence of their old group. Self-differentiation is only in its very early stages. They may have a vague recognition of needing a safe haven and secure base, but this is undefined. Emotional hope is beginning to appear, as is the need for serious cognitive engagement. By this time, the former members may have experienced some unconditional positive regard from a few people (e.g., pre-group friends, supportive relatives, or counselors). These nonmember group relationships are appearing but are undeveloped and may not be very helpful till the next stage. Former members' self-defined identity is in its very early stages and their beliefs are in flux, but they seldom consider those beliefs important. Emotional dysregulation is still a significant challenge, and meeting their daily physical needs is their focus. Depending on available resources, education about the influence of their birth family may not start for years(see Family Systems resources in Appendix C).

Stage 4

The fourth stage of the recovery process is identifiable by increased, yet largely uninformed efforts by former members to *identify a relationally based support recovery team*. This is the core stage of recovery, which is particularly difficult for former members because they are both struggling to know what comprises healthy relationships and risking finding such relationships. Self-differentiation has clearly begun.

Former members' cognitive engagement is advancing and in need of well-informed relational support for them to progress. With the addition of relational connections that offer unconditional positive regard, they are finally beginning to experience emotional peace and regulation. Their efforts for improved cognition and for regulated emotions are both progressing, largely in proportion to their success in having healthy relationships.

At this point, former members' previously held group beliefs are increasingly challenged, and replacement beliefs are appearing. Insights that connect the influence of their respective birth families to the relational dynamics of the abusive group may be emerging. The process of meeting their daily practical needs is well under way.

Stage 5

Depending on their success in finding a secure base relationship, former members in the fifth stage are now passionately *exploring and discovering the world* outside their previous group. Their emotions are more regulated as the result of a reduction of cognitive acedia, and both areas of growth lead to further success in their altruistic efforts.

Improved self-differentiation is evident. The relational world of these former members has significantly expanded and become healthier. With improved positive relationships, their identity is developing. Their beliefs have been significantly reshaped and now include both essential and nonessential dogmas. This process, in turn, allows them to experience improved emotional and cognitive toleration of others.

Fulfilling their needs associated with the daily life is progressing well for these former members; but depending on the level of damage they experienced in the abusive group, they may still need extended time to recover fully in this regard. Their relational growth now includes greater receptivity to exploring family-of-origin influences.

Stage 6

Stage 6 for former members consists of *preserving their recovery and struggling with tendencies to offer excessive support to others.* Their heightened altruistic success can easily result in their being overcommitted and overly responsible for others. Their ability to self-differentiate has advanced significantly. They are deeply involved in cognitive and emotional growth.

The relational world of former members at this stage consists of both their having and offering to others the experience of a safe haven and secure base. Their identity and newly reshaped belief system are both becoming quite clear. Their daily practical needs are mostly being met, and they may now be actively seeking education about the influence of their birth family and its place in their recovery. Former members at this stage have sufficiently recovered to offer informed support to others, albeit disproportionate at times. They continue to actively work on their own ongoing recovery needs.

Stage 7

The seventh stage of recovery from a spiritually abusive group is characterized by former members being *able to offer a consistent, empathetic, and well-informed holding environment* for other former members, and to effect positive changes in their birth family. At this stage, the former members are effectively altruistic and highly self-differentiated, and they have a growing and strong self-identity. Unlike in Stage 6, they are readily able to set altruistic boundaries to meet their own various needs. Both their own belief system and their ability to effectively critique other beliefs are well shaped. They have clearly defined life goals and purpose. Their emotions are stable, and most of their daily practical needs likely have been met.

At this stage, former members easily identify, and appreciate, healthy relationships. They have a strong relational support system that, in turn, allows them to successfully provide other former members the benefits of a safe haven and secure base. They have a passion for ongoing cognitive and emotional education, and they realize that recovery from religious abuse is a life-long adventure. They understand and appreciate the relevancy of their birth family to their religious abuse, and they encourage others to be informed of this connection.

As suggested previously, recognizing and understanding these seven stages in the process of recovery enables those in supportive roles to better prioritize recovery activities to shape an individual plan. The next and final section of this chapter briefly summarizes the strengths and limitations of other approaches and affirms SECURE using the same four questions previously applied to the earlier perspectives of recovery from religious abuse (see chapter 3).

Section 4: SECURE—Advanced

It feels redemptive to use my experiences of, and thoughts about, religious abuse recovery to contribute to this field of cultic studies. This fourth section includes a summary of the strengths and limitations of the detailed evaluations discussed in chapter 3 as they relate to the various perspectives of religious abuse. This summary is followed by an advancement of the SECURE perspective through application of my responses to the four apologetic questions originally presented in chapter 2.

Thought-Reform/Mind-Control Perspective

The thought-reform/mind-control perspective seldom includes the importance of worldview. When one addresses philosophical categories, those groupings commonly include evolutionary naturalist or deistic assumptions and default to an impersonal universe. This approach limits the secular thought-reform perspective; consequently, the approach may be improved in proportion to its consistency with a Christian worldview. Many former members provide strong testimony in support of the thought-reform position; others suggest different views of their religious abuse. Supportive empirical studies for thought reform are rare, and the conclusions based on theoretical research and psychological investigation are diverse; and the varied evidence from general revelation neither strongly supports nor discounts the thought-reform perspective.

From the thought-reform approach, addressing emotions is important in recovery from religious abuse, but the focus on meeting recovery needs is typically through education about the controlling behavioral dynamics integral to the abuse. When driven by a secular worldview, thought-reform avoids the concept of redemptive profit, preferring instead a perceived value-neutral term, *recovery*. This perspective limits the primary benefits to such things as relief from the abusive environment, corrective emotional resiliency, generally improved strength of character, and occasional success in litigation against abusive groups. The degree and diversity of any redemptive profit in recovery within the thought-reform approach is largely determined by the worldview in which it is understood.

Deliberative or Conversionist Conceptualization

When secularly framed, the deliberative or Conversionist approach defaults to some form of naturalism or a deism contrary to a Christian worldview. For both secular and theologically inconsistent Christian adherents, the Conversionist view has two substantial weaknesses. One weakness relates to a false theological view aboutan autonomy of the will and incorporates an inadequate understanding of human responsibility (Wright, R. K. M., 1996, pp. 43–62). The second limitation is the reductive claim that the lack of theological or social education is the primary cause of religious abuse, and that improved education is the principle source of recovery.

Further, the deliberative perspective has been recently weakened by a shift in theoretical investigations and research. Support coming from biographic or autobiographic accounts for the Conversionist perspective is mixed. Corroboration from general revelation of the deliberative approach seems weak when compared to that of other perspectives (see chapter 3). The emphasis on documented facts about beliefs (Christian) and behavior (secular) within the Conversionist view provides an imbalanced primacy over concerns about emotional health.

Both secular and Christian adherents of the Conversionist perspective affirm that the greatest profit that experience in religiously abusive environments might offer is the resulting life education. Those coming from a secular understanding define this profit sociologically, while those from a Christian perspective suggest the improved discernment of true spirituality for the abused as the primary profit. As with all the varying perspectives, philosophical assumptions largely determine how one understands the benefits from an experience of religious abuse.

Psychosocial, Needs-Based Understanding

When secularly understood, the psychosocial, needs-based perspective defaults to a worldview consistent with naturalism or deism. Christian adherents to the psychosocial perspective seem to affirm a consistent biblical worldview. One of the greatest strengths inherent in the psychosocial approach, for both secular and Christian viewpoints, is that it affirms psychosocial terms and concepts as important in describing the perspective. The supportive weight of general revelation for the psychosocial perspective originates from abundant theoretical research, and from the credibility granted the researchers based on their higher levels of education. Some proponents may infer as evidence of the validity of this view its increased popularity.

The greatest weakness of this approach is the lack of autobiographical support, but overall the evidential support from general revelation is strong (see chapter 3). The psychosocial perspective emphasizes the emotional world of former members in their recovery. Compared to other approaches, the important role of emotion in this view is a particular strength. Within a secular approach, the resulting profit from a religiously abusive experience is primarily the fulfillment of psychosocial needs. In both secular and Christian viewpoints, recovery includes healing from trauma and emergence of the authentic, or true self. Depending on the worldview, the potential profit derived from religious abuse can be considerable and significantly strengthens the value of the psychosocial perspective.

Dynamic-Systems Approach

When secularly defined, the dynamic-systems approach affirms a naturalistic or deistic worldview that can easily default to a broad, secular existentialism devoid of a transcendent, holy, personal, and sovereign God as found in the Bible. When Christian assumptions are included, as evidenced primarily in the writings of some addiction theorists, the result often supports the Bible's view of reality. Both secular and Christian concepts of the dynamic-systems approach are holistic, and adherents of both perspectives are more willing than those with other perspectives to consider the importance of one's worldview. The growth of general systems theory has given rise to family-systems therapy(see related Family Systems resources in Appendix C). This has in turn, resulted in some exploring of the correlation between the family system, and religious abuse (Aguado, 2018; Sirkin, 1990; Wickliff, 1989). Compared to other perspectives, much empirical and theoretical research remains to be done to validate this approach. Supportive autobiographic or biographic evidence from former member accounts is rare. The dynamic-systems approach identifies the importance of the relational system of influence. It has grown in popularity but is still weak in general revelation support(see chapter 3). The therapeutic attention often defaults to the operational system, rather than the importance of emotion. A strength of the dynamic-systems approach is the integrated epistemic lens through which it operates and that is not found in other perspectives. When relational systems are shaped by a Christian worldview, the result is a clear interconnectedness that includes a personal God, which those systems otherwise do not consider. The greatest strength of the dynamic-systems prospective, particularly when understood within a Christian worldview, is how easily it affirms that past experiences of abuse can be redemptive.

Each of these four perspectives, in their conceptions of recovery from religious or spiritual abuse, have made significant contributions to the field of cultic studies. It is also true that each has limitations based on both the current lack of empirical and theoretical support, and their accompanying worldviews.

The SECURE Approach

The SECURE approach is a family systems perspective informed by a Christian worldview through which one can understand religious abuse and recovery. Application of the essential principles of SECURE affirms the strengths of the previously identified perspectives, avoids their limitations, and improves the context for understanding religious abuse recovery (Appendix B). I now advance the SECURE approach by answering the previously identified four apologetic questions.

SECURE: Question 1.

The first question is a worldview inquiry that centers on the underlying axiom of Christianity, special revelation: "To what degree does the particular approach affirm the Bible's perspective in the six philosophical categories of prime reality, teleology, anthropology, ethics, epistemology and semantics?" The answer to this question provides the epistemological basis for assessing the value of various approaches to religious abuse and recovery. This question identifies the standard or criteria for all that follows. In philosophic vernacular, this question is basic or foundational, and assists in determining the cogency of responses to the other three questions.

The essential recovery principle of a safe haven and a secure base is universal to human experience as identified in the Bible. God Himself provides the most secure of secure relationships (Ps 46:1, 7, 11). This relationship with Him imparts a gratitude that motivates and empowers us to offer security and love for others (1 John 4:19). This God is a personal being (Deut 6:4) and exists as a plurality of persons (2 Cor 13:14; Matt 28:19; Matt 3:16–17). Christians understand God as a tripersonal eternal being, referred to as the Trinity—Father, Son, and Holy Spirit. Many Christian theologians have identified the importance of the Trinitarian doctrine of God and encouraged a consistent theology in general (see related Theology resources in Appendix C).

SECURE places a high value on healthy relationships, both among humans and with the Creator, because these relationships are the primary means for optimal healing from religious abuse. We are relational creatures because we derive our being from the *prime reality* of the omniscient yet personal God of the Bible (Acts 17:28), through whom all of life is properly understood: "For with you is the fountain of life [knowledge is possible], in your light, [God's self-disclosure], we see light [we understand reality]" (Ps 36:9). Based in His ground of being, God's teleology includes a four-fold, unique plan of redemption: grace (Eph 2:8–9), forgiveness (John 3:16), love (1 John 4:7–21), and justice (Deut 32:4; Isa 61:8; Rom 12:19).

SECURE strongly affirms that we are all made in God's likeness. Consequently, we know Him, both in the experience of our own being, and in relationship with others. As the Creator, and ultimate judge of all things, God and His ethics understandably define ours (Lev 19:13; John 13:34–35). Applying the SECURE approach, we believe we can know God's desire for our behavior, at least in principle, through the means He has arranged. His chosen methods by which we obtain knowledge are special revelation—holy scripture (2 Tim 3:15–17; Heb 1:1–2), and general revelation (Ps 19:1–2; Rom 1:20). The Bible itself assumes the knowledge of God, meaningfully communicated through knowable statements (Gen 1:1; John 1:1–5). The SECURE perspective seeks the careful use of words and concepts because of their potential to make known the prime reality of God (Prov 2:1–5; Ps 119:105; 2 Tim 3:15–17; Matt 4:4). Finally, SECURE supports the idea that all of our natural associations among the disciplines of theology, philosophy, the arts, sociology, psychology, history, and culture, rather than running in "unrelated parallel lines," are instead understood as a well-designed, personal, cohesive unity (Schaeffer, 1968, p. 12).

Unlike most other perspectives of recovery from religious abuse, SE-CURE clearly identifies this designed unity found in scripture (John 1:1–5). This philosophic or theological structure is found in the principles of SE-CURE, agrees with the Bible's theological view of reality, and therefore provides a unique context within which optimal recovery can be understood.

SECURE: Question 2

The second key question focuses on the evidence for SECURE found in general revelation: "What is the supporting evidence found in history, psychosocial research, and general life experience or the natural world as affirmed or denied from within each of the four perspectives?"

This question seeks to determine the evidence of general revelation found in each approach. The answer to the Question 1 suggests that evidence found in history is not isolated or unrelated, but instead is ultimately understood as coming from the Creator, the God of the Bible. If that is true, then it is reasonable to assume that natural evidence found in theoretical and empirical psychosocial research and in autobiographic accounts would likely support the essential principles of SECURE and a Christian worldview. Christians are not expected to affirm a *blind faith*, but a reasonable faith, one that includes supportive natural evidence (Ps 19; Acts 14:17; Rom 1–2).

The six essential principles of SECURE (see Appendix B) are clearly identified and verified in the psychosocial research. Recent attachment investigation also supports the important concepts of a safe haven and a secure base asessential to relational health (Reisz, Brennan, Jacobvitz, & George, 2019). Additionally, there is abundant empirical support for the importance of working directly with emotions as a primary means to relational growth and healing (see related Attachment/EFT resources in Appendix C). The importance of reversing cognitive acedia is upheld in our culture's dominant counseling modality of cognitive behavioral therapy. Some professionals even refer to cognitive behavioral therapy as the "gold standard" in psychotherapy (David, Cristea, & Hoffman, 2018). Additionally, the essential SECURE principle of providing unconditional positive regard is widely accepted today in person-centered approaches to therapy (Hazler, 2016). Understood within a Christian worldview (Clark, D. K., 1993), this principle of unconditional positive regard as defined biblically (see Appendix A) is essential to the SECURE perspective. The supportive empirical research regarding the general magnitude of past harmful family dynamics and the value of improving family relationships is abundant (see related "Family Systems/Empirical Research" resources in Appendix C). However, this issue is yet to be fully explored within the specific context of religious abuse. Meanwhile, the value of relational support for trauma recovery is well documented (Herman, 2015; see also Trauma Recoveryresources in Appendix C). Finally, the application of general systems theory to relational systems has grown since the appearance of family systems theory, and it continues to gain therapeutic relevance to recovery from religious abuse (Aguado, 2018).

Meanwhile, the supportive biographic/autobiographic evidence for SECURE remains largely to be seen. Few of those who have been spiritually abused have provided personal testimony that supports the correlation between family-of-origin dynamics and the relational dynamics in religious-abuse environments (Knapp, P., 1998). Currently, this is the weakest of evidential support for SECURE. Possible reasons for this lack of evidence are identified in chapter 5. Meanwhile, the weight of general revelation still provides strong confirmation for the SECURE approach; but as with the other four perspectives, SECURE has room for growth.

SECURE: Question 3

The third question highlights the degree to which the emotional life of a person is valued (emotional affirmation): "What can one identify in each perspective that encourages the emotional health of former members and offers a deeper understanding of religious or spiritual abuse?"

The essential recovery principle of granting emotion a prominent role in healing from religious abuse is identified in the first *E* of SECURE. As evidenced in my own recovery and found in the recovery of others, working directly with emotions is essential to heal religious abuse. As previously addressed, former members are dominated by the challenge of emotional disequilibrium following such abuse. This response is evidenced by emotional triggers that reveal the need for recovery. Emotional growth also can provide healing in other areas not otherwise attained (see Attachment/EFT resources in Appendix C). SECURE incorporates a high regard for the integration of emotion and cognition to address psychological needs.

The highly respected and empirically supported Emotion Focused Therapy (EFT; see the Attachment/EFT resources in Appendix C) has principles easily identified in SECURE. Crediting Greenberg (2004) for them, Ackerman (2017) noted that among these principles are the importance of emotions

- in attachment and relational bonding;
- as the basis for how "we construct our very selves";
- for "communicating intentions to others and regulating interactions";
- for "inform[ing] decision making; and
- for alerting one to threats; and
- as a help in goal setting. (Ackerman, 2017, paras. 4–5)

The SECURE approach puts a high value on the emotional life of those influenced by religious abuse; doing otherwise disrespects the individual made in the image of God, who Himself clearly values emotions and the many benefits they provide. Bruce Baloian, Professor Emeritus at the Department of Biblical and Religious Studies, Azusa Pacific, biblically affirmed this thinking when he stated the following:

> One of the dominant impressions the ascribing of anger to Yahweh has, is to present Him as an intense and passionate Being, fervently interested in the world of humans. There is no embarrassment on the part of the OT [Old Testament] of Yahweh's possession of emotion, but rather, it is celebrated (see for example, 2 Sam 22:8, 9, 16; Ps 145:8). In fact, His passion guarantees, not only that He is intensely interested in the word [emotion], but that He is a person [described as having emotion] (Baloian, 1992, p. 156).

It is because God chose to describe Himself as an emotional being that addressing emotion is particularly important in the process of recovery from religious abuse. This value of emotion is reinforced in the New Testament records of the divine person of Christ (John 10:30; 14:9). Well-known are Jesus's passionate emotions: John 2:13–17; 11:35; Luke 10:21; Matt 26:36–38; and finally, we see his intense anguish expressed at his death, Matt 27:45–50. The God of the Bible places a high regard on emotion, and so too must perspectives of recovery from religious abuse. SECURE understands this value and therefore requires that a paced or measured response be given to the next and final question of redemptive profit.

SECURE: Question 4

The answer to this final question identifies the positive value (redemptive profit) derived from the negative experience of religious abuse and recovery: "In the course of developing one's understanding of recovery from religious or spiritual abuse, in what ways do each of the four perspectives affirm that substantial and meaningful redemption is obtainable?"

This is commonly the most emotionally charged and difficult apologetic question, both for those influenced by religious abuse and for those writing about its recovery. This question occurs last because it requires answers to the philosophical and practical concerns of the first three questions.

It is easy to acknowledge the profits from religious abuse previously identified in the earlier discussion of the other recovery perspectives (see chapter 3). God is lovingly active in meeting the recovery needs of the religiously abused (Matt 23). However, in addition, SECURE offers a theological context that ensures a redemptive profit that is more consistently hopeful and more inclusive than typically found in the other four perspective of recovery from religious abuse.

Those who have been influenced by religious abuse often have questions of their own about redemptive profit, and they typically do not find answers to these questions until sometime in the sixth or seventh stage of recovery. Instead, their questions about redemption are *Why* questions—"Why did this religious abuse *ultimately* take place?" Or, depending on a former member's particular abusive group, and especially if the individual came from a TACO—"Why did God allow this? Why didn't He just prevent me from joining? Did He, in some sense, cause it? And if so, why?"

These questions about God and ultimate meaning, which are often heard from those impacted by religious abuse, are the hardest to answer and require the most time, reflection, personal care, and helpful timing. To help them recover from their sense of lost time, money, relationships, and life opportunities, those influenced by religious abuse want answers to these questions to give them maximum redemptive profit. As a consequence, the answer offered here is much longer than given for the first three questions in this section of the chapter. Rather than see Question 4 subsumed under the general and generic category of *recovery*, I prefer the unique biblical view of profitable redemption. That view includes both redemptive profits discovered during one's life and, more fully, the liberating profit that the Bible promises through eternity.

The Bible provides a unique meta-narrative of redemption—everything from the first redemptive promise following the Fall of Adam and Eve (Gen 3:15), to the final events of our world and beyond (Rev 21–22). The Bible is a book of redemption and therefore can be a source of hope and encouragement for those influenced by religious abuse. However, former members may initially consider the importance of such a meta-narrative as irrelevant or too emotionally triggering. I briefly consider the reasons for this in chapter 5.

A first level of response to the redemption question may come relatively easily. It may be something like,"We all live in an imperfect world. Sadly, hurtful, religiously motivated things happen to us. They are painful, but we can learn from those experiences." This early basic response is similar to what might one might offer to another in the first stages of recovery, together with providing the principles of thought reform, and then eventually graduating to the topic of negative birth-family influences. Over the course of time, within safe relationships and the emotional healing process, the idea of obtaining a profound, profitable redemption that includes a loving and sovereign God becomes more palatable to the abused and can be more easily addressed. Former members may desire to look deeper, to a grand philosophical or theological meaning that includes meaning and purpose both within this life and the afterlife, and that brings a more comprehensive sense of redemption to their experience of religious abuse.

This deeper-level answer of redemptive profit is seldom recognized in other perspectives of religious abuse and recovery. The God of the Bible as identified in SECURE provides more than consolation or repair. Instead, the recovering persons' pain and suffering leads them to an increased understanding of God not otherwise attained (e.g., Joseph, in Gen 34–50; Job, in Job 42:1–6; and the man born blind, in John 9). This view does not imply, as some may suggest, that God is the author of evil (Wright, R. K. M., 1996, pp. 177–204), but that He personally and actively predetermines a particular result or end, both for His ultimate glory, and for the good of His children (Rom 8:28). Coming to such a conclusion is understandably difficult, and it seldom comes quickly. Coming to such a conclusion can, over time, help those influenced by religious abuse find optimal recovery, be able to trust in the God of the Bible, and grow in their relationship with Him, rather than default to previous, false ideas of God and spirituality.

Religious abuse is evil. But in the hands of a loving and sovereign God, it can also become an ultimate means for one to discover the source of relational security, feel emotionally affirmed, reduce cognitive acedia, experience unconditional acceptance, actively participate in healthy relationships, and heal from the negative contributions of one's family of origin. When framed within a Christian worldview, these six areas of recovery are found in the principles of SECURE and afford a unique level of redemptive profit supported by noteworthy examples of past Christian leaders.

Jonathan Edwards, famous Protestant pastor, and one of the influences with the greatest impact in the First Great Awakening (see chapter 1), wrote an influential book concerning redemption (Edwards, J., 1774/2003). In this text, he concluded that everything in human history, from start to finish, is subservient to the unthwarted work of Christ's redemption, everything that occurs serves to advance that redemption, and is for our ultimate profit. During this same time period, the writings of John Newton reflect similar conclusions about the benefits of redemptive suffering and pain (https://www.monergism.com/benefits-affliction). Newton, the author of the Christian hymn *Amazing Grace*(1779), endured much personal pain and, as a slave-trader prior to his conversion, had imposed great suffering on others. Other historic examples that support such personal redemptive profit are found throughout history (see related Redemptive Stories resources in Appendix C). Also—as suggested in the words of Anglican writer C. S. Lewis (Lewis, C. S., 1946): "Heaven, once attained, will work backwards and turn even that agony [all pain and suffering] into a glory" (p. 64)—redemption may be found not only within our current state, but also in the afterlife.

Presenting at an ICSA conference on healing marital wounds caused by religious abuse, Heidi Knapp (2018) suggested that these truths about redemptive profit might be concretely and creatively conveyed. She did so using an illustration drawn from the ancient and beautiful Japanese art form of Kintsugi (see https://mymodernmet.com/kintsugi-kintsukuroi).

This creative form of art involves fixing broken pottery with a special lacquer that consists of powered gold or other metals, which results in a unique appearance with improved utility, beauty, and value. The artisan uses all the broken pieces; none are discarded or devalued. Similarly, the various areas of personal brokenness caused by religious abuse are not only repaired by the resourceful Artist (the God of the Bible), but may result, through creative means, in a uniquely beautiful life: "We are his [artistic] workmanship" (Eph 2:10). I believe that the Bible supports the idea that absolutely nothing experienced in a religiously abusive environment is to be wasted but, over time, may be viewed as redemptive profit. There are no chance events in God's universe because He is sovereign (Ps 115:3; Eph 1:11, 21–23) and capable of using all things to bring about His desired ends.

Finally, two combined thoughts—one from Catholic fiction writer J. R. R. Tolkien (1965, p. 283), and one from Presbyterian pastor Timothy Keller (2014)—suggest a maximum level of redemptive benefit to creatively answer this apologetic question. In Tolkien's (1965) *The Lord of the Rings—The Return of the King (Part Three)*, Sam (an adventurous hobbit), who has just experienced what felt like death, turns to Gandalf (a wise wizard and traveling companion) and states, "I thought you were dead! But then I thought I was dead myself. Is everything sad going to come untrue?" As an avid Tolkien fan, Keller takes Sam's heartfelt question and answers it, providing a biblically redemptive response in a succinct statement, "Everything sad is going to become untrue, and it will somehow be greater for having once been broken and lost" (Keller, 2014). Although this may seem a radical answer, it has been echoed throughout human history and is SECURE's response to substantial meaningful redemption.

The SECURE approach affirms the previously identified perspectives in the form of their greatest strengths: thought-reform view, which provides early education about the imposed manipulative behaviors of others; the deliberative approach, which stresses the importance of beliefs and developmental growth; the psychosocial perspective, which affirms the value and role of emotion; the dynamic-systems approach, which emphasizes the importance of the relational system of influence, and of viewing religious abuse and recovery as a holistic system.

At the same time, the SECURE perspective avoids the notable limitations of each of the other viewpoints: the thought-reform view, with its overfocus on others' behaviors; the deliberative approach, which marginalizes emotion; the psychosocial perspective, with its limitation of redemptive profit when not understood from a Christian worldview; and the dynamic-systems approach, with its overemphasis on the system of abuse rather than the individual role and value of emotion. SECURE also offers an improved context, with an unambiguously defined Christian worldview consistent with the Bible and significant evidence from general revelation; demonstrates the important role of emotions; and values the unique redemptive profit found in the Bible, and not clearly identified in the other four perspectives of religious abuse and recovery.

In this chapter, I have introduced, illustrated, and advocated for SE-CURE, an alternative approach to religious abuse and recovery (see Appendix B). Section 1 includes a description of six essential principles of recovery; Section 2, an identification of eight core recovery needs and suggested reparative activities; Section 3, an outline of seven recovery stages in the process of healing; and finally, Section 4, a brief summary of the strengths and limitations of other approaches and an advancement of the SECURE perspective using the same four evaluative questions previously applied to the other approaches. In the next, and final, chapter, I suggest some of the remaining research, development, and practical concerns that may be helpful to further our understanding of and promote recovery from religious abuse.

5

Remaining Research
and Development (SECURE)

IN THE PREVIOUS CHAPTER, I introduced, illustrated, and advanced a new, alternative approach to recovery from religious abuse. The essential principles of SECURE (Appendix B) affirm the previously identified perspectives in their strengths, avoid their limitations, and provide an improved context for understanding religious abuse and recovery. This final chapter contains a discussion of the remaining research and development that may benefit cultic studies generally and further advance the SECURE approach. Recommended are seven influential areas for developmental growth:

a. Increase the *acceptance of a theologically consistent Christian worldview* to improve the conceptual theory and therapeutic practice for recovery from religious abuse.

b. Implement *new applications of empirical research* to measure the correlation of family-of-origin systems and one's involvement in religiously abusive environments.

c. Advance *education on family systems theory* to better support biographic and autobiographic evidence in favor of the SECURE perspective.

d. Encourage the growth in *psychosocial and spiritual formation* of those working with the recovery needs of the religiously abused to better model maturity and health.

e. Publish *popular literature in support of the essential principles of the SECURE perspective* to broadly promote the approach.

f. Explore the *application of emotion-focused therapy* to meet the attachment needs of those affected by religious abuse.

g. Support *integrative approaches to cultic studies* that value an interdisciplinary outlook to encourage a systematic, holistic clarity about religious abuse and recovery not otherwise easily attained.

A discussion of these topics of developmental growth and research follows. This discussion includes suggestions about who may best contribute to these areas to advance cultic studies generally and promote and further shape the SECURE perspective specifically.

Acceptance of a Theologically Consistent Christian Worldview

The SECURE perspective acknowledges the essential function of a theologically consistent Christian worldview to bring optimal recovery (see chapter 2). Also assumed is a correspondence view of truth, "the claim that a true statement is one that agrees with or matches the reality it describes" (Groothuis, 2000, p. 13). In our present postmodern culture, and within the secular arm of cultic studies, support for a correspondence view of truth has diminished, largely replaced by naturalist or broadly deist worldviews that deny the role of the God of the Bible (chapter 2). This limitation, denying the Christian God His rightful place in spiritual formation and psychosocial growth, is also exemplified in compromises made by many leaders in the Christian church.

It is widely accepted in cultic studies that most religious or spiritual abuse comes from groups that are *Bible based* (see Appendix A for a definition, and chapter 1 for the supportive history). This perspective primarily results from teachings of errant beliefs about the necessity of leaders exercising absolute authority over others in the church (e.g., Nee, 1972); the failure of these teachings to promote authentic forms of Christian spirituality that counter an overemphasis on subjective experiences (Johnson, A., 1988); and finally, minimization of the importance of church history (see chapter 1). Many conservative Christian philosophers and theologians voice the need to reverse this trend (see Pastoral/Cultural Influences Upon the Church resources in Appendix C), but church leadership is largely silent. This silence suggests that the Christian church, particularly in the West, may currently be in an unhealthy condition, which by default contributes more to the problem of religious abuse than it offers in support of recovery. A more receptive or flexible Christian church leadership might find positive influence from thoughtful Christian philosophers and theologians. This approach would offer more hope for reversing the postmodern cultural flow that rejects objective truth and succumbs to a self-referential autonomy that denies the authority of scripture and it's "rational knowability" (Groothuis, 2000, pp. 111–38). Valuing such an influence could help reduce the presence of religious abuse and better offer support for those recovering from abusive groups. Church leaders can also take the time and make the effort to learn from the best of their own leadership in making their religious institutions safe havens for the religiously abused (Damgaard, 2015). Learning from others, these church leaders can also become aware of a broad range of resources that are tailor-made for ministry to the spiritually abused (see Pastoral resources in Appendix C).

When interacting with former members, particularly from TACOs, church leaders can help identify sound hermeneutical principles for interpreting the Bible (for related resources, see Appendix B). Perhaps most importantly, they can resist "fixing" those damaged by religious abuse, and instead take the time to ask thoughtful questions, listen deeply, and resist giving unhelpful, naïve responses. They can acknowledge the reality of religious abuse and the various recovery needs, suggesting not only supportive resources but also model their own best example of loving care and patience. Such changes in their behavior, their theological understanding, and their willingness to glean lessons from history could help church leadership establish a cognitive and behavioral shift both to benefit culticstudies broadly and in support of the SECURE perspective specifically.

New Applications of Empirical Research

To my knowledge, there has been no empirical testing to measure the correlation between family-of-origin relational systems and individuals' involvement in religiously abusive environments. The reasons for this lack may be diverse: avoiding such research may offer easily acceptable, reductionist answers to complex problems; facing significant past family problems may feel overwhelming; additionally, most of those writing about religious abuse and recovery seem to be generally unfamiliar with the field of family therapy and, in particular, to avoid the important place of habituated roles, rules, and boundaries as identified in some segments of addictions theory (Knapp, P., 2000, pp. 96–100; see also chapter 4).

But empirical testing to measure the functional health of a family is available (for related resources, see Family Systems/Empirical Research resources in Appendix C) and could be thoughtfully applied to those previously affected by religious abuse. Employing such testing will obviously require several converging components, including choosing the most empirically verified tests; selecting the appropriate timing to conduct the testing; involving well-informed testing administrators; ensuring the essential support from former members and their families; and finally, publishing, by those most qualified to interpret the findings, the appropriate and objective empirical results.

Education on Family Systems Theory

The application of systems theory to businesses and churches has become widely accepted in our culture (see Appendix C). As mentioned in chapter 4, the value of family systems theory is well-accepted in the field of addictions recovery. Education that ties together the importance of seeing life as a relational system, and specifically, the dynamics of family relationships as a foundation for understanding religious abuse and recovery, could provide tremendous strength to the general field of cultic studies. With my encouragement and input, one of the first published articles by a family therapist suggested a correlation between religiously abusive systems and dysfunctional families (Aguado, 2018). The involvement of other therapeutic innovators may bring improved understanding of family systems theory and alter biographic and autobiographic evidence in favor of the SECURE perspective.

Psychosocial and Spiritual Formation

For those in the helping professions, personal and family needs often are marginalized in favor of meeting the needs of clients. With the pressing recovery needs of the religiously abused (chapter 4, section 2), the psychological and spiritual needs of the supportive healers and their own loved ones can easily go unmet. Working with former members and their families has informed me that who I am as a person, a spouse, and a parent can sometimes speak louder than my expressed ideas, beliefs, and theories about religious abuse and recovery. To be encouraged, to find hope, and perhaps even to emulate them, former members and their families need to see models of those who seek ever-increasing psychosocial and spiritual health. Modeling a life well-lived can help to advance one's theories in a way that lectures and published research may not.

Most of those persons working in this recovery field are themselves recovering former members, many of whom are in Stage 5 or Stage 6 of the recovery process (see chapter 4, section 3). Having worked hard to provide support to other former members and their families, they may have had considerable success in helping others, but yet they are in need of their own further recovery. The adage *You can't give what you don't have* is often affirmed within addictions recovery and is applicable to recovery from religious abuse. Helping professionals who become more open and committed to their own psychosocial and spiritual health not only encourage their own families, friends, and peers, but also provide examples of what a truly healthy person might become. In this context, specific programs, articles, and books might be designed for cultic-studies professionals to support them in developing their own psychosocial and spiritual health.

Popular Literature on the SECURE Perspective

Often, the people most receptive to reading about recovery from religious abuse are former members, their families, and the general population. While I hope this book has an impact in advocating for the SECURE perspective for those professionals in cultic-studies, I also hope to produce popular literature that has a more jargon-free, readable, and passionately written approach, with creative use of metaphors, to bring broader support for the approach. I have published several small articles promoting the various concepts behind SECURE, but I have yet to produce a larger, user-friendly, book version. Following completion of this book and drawing from it, I plan to publish such a book that specifically targets the general readership. Additionally, Heidi Knapp and I are currently drafting a daily devotional publication for the spiritually abused; and we continue to develop other various projects, including formal presentations that further explore and advance portions of the SECURE approach.

Application of Emotion-Focused Therapy

In chapter 4, section 1, I stressed the importance of working directly with the emotions of those who have experienced religious abuse. Examples of the application of this approach in the field of recovery from spiritual abuse are increasing: The application of attachment theory to addressing the recovery needs of those spiritually abused has recently been suggested in a chapter entitled "Mentalization Attachment Approach to Cult Recovery," in *Cult Recovery: A Clinician's Guide* (Henry, 2017, pp. 117–38). Emotion-focused therapy (EFT), derived from attachment theory, has increased in popularity in the field of counseling theory and practice. EFT is both an empirically verified, successful form of marriage therapy (see Attachment/EFT resources in Appendix C) and is strongly supported by others in the general field of counseling.

The popularity of this relatively new form of therapy also was evident in a recent (2017) American Association of Christian Counselors (AACC) conference (with more than six thousand persons in attendance). The AACC is the largest organization of Christian counselors in the world (see www.aacc.net). In its September 2017 world conference, Heidi Knapp and I spoke briefly with Dr. Sue Johnson, the primary founder of EFT, and the AACC's keynote speaker. We shared with her our passion of working with those in need of healing from religious abuse. She was very sympathetic and interested in our work, and she asked many thoughtful questions. Because EFT is primarily focused on the use and benefit of individuals working directly with their emotions to recover from various forms of relational injury, it stands to reason that this approach may be applied in some form to recovery from religious abuse. Sue Johnson, along with Kenneth Sanderfer (Johnson, S., & Sanderfer, 2016), have recently adapted Johnson's EFT principles to comport with a Christian worldview clearly found in scripture. An innovative step to further develop SECURE may be to explore the possible applications of attachment principles and practices of EFT to recovery from religious abuse. To begin this exploration, I have made recent attempts to reach out to both the AACC and the literary agent for Dr. Sue Johnson to explore possible future publishing and conference-presentation efforts.

Integrative Approaches to Cultic Studies

My intention for this book is that it be an example of an interdisciplinary perspective of religious abuse and recovery, and that it encourage a systematic, holistic clarity on the topic within cultic studies that otherwise has not yet been attained. In a complex field in which myopic focus often results in fragmented formulations, contributions from sociology, philosophy, theology, church history, and psychology are needed to achieve this theoretical unity. Additionally, inevitable cross-pollination among these fields may stimulate new ideas and help reduce the ambiguity on the topic. Interdisciplinary, collegial dialogue canlead tointegrated research and writing efforts, which in turn may yield a larger, more supportive and inclusive system that reflects a greater understanding ofand appreciation forthe process of healing from religious abuse. The research and developmental needs of cultic studies and for the SECURE perspective are many and necessarily include a diverse mix of collaborating contributors. Such efforts influence cultic studies in general and the approach of the SECURE perspective in particular.

As I reflect on the recovery struggles of former members and their families, I am reminded of those in the United Kingdom who sought encouragement during and following World War II. Toward the end of this war, Winston Churchill, one of our greatest world leaders, aptly stated, "This is not the end. It is not even the beginning of the end. But it is, perhaps, the end of the beginning" (Churchill, 1942). Like Winston Churchill, I too hope for victory, continued recovery for myself, and for the healing of others affected by religious abuse. Unlike Churchill, I do not expect to make the impact on history he evidently intended; but, with a particular focus on the spiritually abused, I do hope to consistently trust and learn from the great Historian and His ability to "bind up the brokenhearted, to proclaim freedom for the captives and release from darkness for the prisoners" (Isa 61:1; see also Luke 4:16–21). Because of the God behind this promise, I believe this book can provide some hope and encouragement to those needing recovery from religious abuse, along with increased insight and resources for those supporting them in their healing journey.

Appendix A

Glossary for the SECURE Approach

Apologetics

From the Greek *apologia* (Acts 22:1, wherein the Apostle Paul makes a defense for the Christian faith among the various philosophers of his day). Apologetics represents the systematic, intellectual discipline of presenting a justification for religious belief (see "Apologetics" resources in Appendix C).

Attachment patterns

Behaviors hardwired from birth and habituated on a continuum, such as the normative behavioral method for acquiring a safe haven and a secure base. Secure attachment patterns reflect comfort with closeness and an expressed need for others. Insecure attachment patterns are understood as anxious, having a protesting response; avoidant, having a distancing response; or disorganized, vacillating between anxious or avoidant responses.

Attachment theory

A developmental personality theory originating with John Bowlby (1969, 1972, 1980, 1982, 1988) on the importance to individuals of social contact, physical proximity, and emotional bonding with those who provide the felt need of a safe haven and a secure base. Originally, the theory was formulated in how mothers and their children interact in times of stress and duress; it has since broadened to include adult relationships.

Appendix A

Autonomous	Within the context of biblical theology, this term refers to an individual's exercise of independence from accountability to the God of the Bible.
Axiom	A proposition regarded as true and self-evident.
Bible-based	A legitimate reference to the Bible that is frequently used erroneously by abusive groups for the purpose of control and manipulation.
Cognitive acedia	A profound indifference to using, or the inability to properly use, one's cognition (mental action or process) to acquire the knowledge necessary to accurately interpret reality.
Correspondence view of truth	Claim that a true statement is one that agrees with or matches the reality it describes.
Countercult:	Term for a social group that opposes a new or different religious movement, most often primarily on theological grounds.
"Creed over deed"	The concept that examining the beliefs of a religious group, rather than examining its behaviors, should be the standard by which to determine its value or health.
Cult	As used in this document, a group that holds to beliefs or practices that clearly contradict the Bible in many of its central teachings, while it promotes a sinful form of dependency on others, especially on its leader.
Cult apologist/ cult sympathizer	One who supports the free rights of all belief systems and commonly minimizes the negative aspects of religiously abusive groups. See also *Procult.*
"Deed over creed"	The concept that examining the behaviors, rather than the beliefs, of a religious group should be the standard to determine its value or health.

Deism	Worldview that acknowledges God as transcendent, impersonal, and the First Cause of the universe, and who then left humankind to fend for itself. Typically, the external world from this view is seen as a mechanical, cause-and-effect, closed system in which miracles do not exist.
Epistemology	Philosophical branch of study that includes the theory and basis of knowledge, particularly in reference to the limits and validity of that knowledge. Sometimes referred to as "the theory of knowledge."
Existential viability	Philosophical concept regarding whether a belief is consistently livable.
Existentialism	Worldview in which reality is definable only by the individual and the individual's choices. This view comes in two forms, atheistic (e.g., Sartre) and theistic (e.g., Kierkegaard).
Floating	Normative mental dissociation caused by a negative emotional trigger resulting from past religious abuse.
General revelation	Evidence found in the world of history, psychosocial science, life experiences, and the natural disclosure of the world around us.
Genogram:	Historical, pictorial display of family relationships intended to increase insight about the presence of multigenerational patterns.
Habituation	Ingrained pattern of a behavior, emotion, or belief that is difficult to change.
Holding environment	A safe and empowering relationship, similar to the concept of a safe haven or a secure base.
Imago Dei	Latin for "made in the likeness, or image of God."
Interventionist/ thought-reform consultant	One who typically is well-informed about mind-control techniques and who assists people in exiting religiously abusive environments.

Love-bombing	Giving an inordinate amount of respect, attention, or deference to individuals, typically during their recruitment into a religiously abusive environment.
Meta-narrative	Large, philosophical picture of life that helps define one's reality.
Metaphysics/ontology	Philosophical discipline in which one examines the existence and nature of things, such as God, humans, matter, and so on.
Mind control/ thought reform	Set of techniques used manipulatively to unethically influence how a person thinks, feels, and acts, with the purpose of creating a detrimental dependency upon another. Also referred to as *coercive persuasion, undue influence.*
New religious movement	Sociological concept commonly used in place of cult that affirms a neutral, rather than derogatory or dismissive, connotation.
Pantheistic monism	Worldview that affirms the oneness and unity of reality, and that reality is in some sense divine and should be revered. This reality is impersonal, exclusively spiritual, and heavily illusory.
Pelagianism	Term comes from Pelagius, a second-century monk who promoted heretical Christian views that denied original sin and promoted an autonomy of the will that was free from God's influence. Pelagianism was the precursor to semi-Pelagianism, and both were condemned as heretical in AD 529.
Polysemic	Use of many different names for the one God.
Postmodernism	Worldview that defines reality only by the social-environmental construct in which one finds oneself, and by the particular self-authenticating language one uses.

Prime reality/ontology	The most basic of philosophical categories and, given consistency in logic, that which determines the definition of reality.
Procult	Description of one who defends or supports a religiously abusive group or person.
Redemptive profit	Christian belief that all pain and suffering eventually results in the very best for Christians and is to the glory of God.
Reductionist	One who oversimplifies a concept or reality.
Reference point/ worldview	One's set of beliefs that ultimately affects how we act.
Safe Haven	Emotionally safe relationship that offers comfort and security in times of stress and duress. Research has shown that this condition most commonly occurs in relationship with the mother or mother figure and results in encoded attachment patterns later in life.
Secure Base	Supportive relationship that encourages one's exploration of the world, creating a sense of personal competence and healthy autonomy. Research has shown this state originates most often through the father or father figure and is embedded to promote particular attachment patterns through life.
Self-differentiation	One's ability to identify the difference between one's own feelings and thoughts, and also to separate others' thoughts and feelings from one's own.
Semi-Pelagianism	Christian theology originating in the fifth century that taught that God's grace was unnecessary for the human will to act rightly. This belief was condemned as heretical at the Second Council of Orange in AD 529 and was a precursor to the Christian theology of Arminianism, which rejected predestination and affirmed the autonomy of the human will.

Special revelation	Refers to the Bible and what it directly teaches or infers by principle.
Syncretism	The attempt to blend together ideas and concepts that do not logically or philosophically mix.
Thought-reform consultant	Individual who assists in the voluntary exit of a member from a religiously abusive group that uses thought-reform techniques to control their membership.
Transference	Unconscious projection of one's attitudes, desires, or aggression upon another person.
Triggers	External or internal sensory cues that create emotional disequilibrium.
Unconditional positive regard	Within a Christian worldview, acknowledgment of the importance of unconditional and nonjudgmental acceptance, trusting individuals' ability to find psychological health as they depend upon God for change to occur (Phil 1:6), and that He is the ultimate source of truth (John 17:17).
Westminster Confession of Faith (1647)	One of the most comprehensive and well-accepted statements of Christian faith in the Reformed tradition.

Appendix B

SECURE—
Essential Recovery Principles

Spheres of Influence

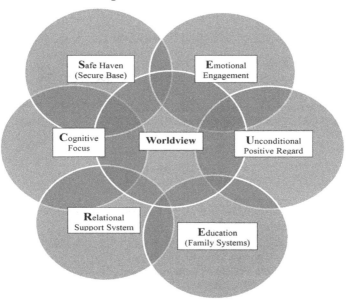

Safe Haven
(Secure Base)

Emotional
Engagement

Cognitive
Focus

Worldview

Unconditional
Positive Regard

Relational
Support System

Education
(Family Systems)

THE CENTER SPHERE CONTAINS the belief system that ultimately influences each of the surrounding six essential spheres. Each activated sphere empowers and affects the others. Over the course of optimal recovery, people are variously willing in differing degrees to engage in each of the spheres. As recovery occurs, their worldview may become more consistent with a Christian perspective as theologically understood from the Bible.

Appendix C

Resources for the SECURE Approach

Addictions

Website Resources

Alcoholics Anonymous. http://www.aa.org.
Center for Dependency, Addiction and Rehabilitation (CeDAR). https://www.
cedarcolorado.org.
Denver Veterans Medical. https://www.denver.va.gov.
Jeff VanVonderen. https://www.jeffvanvonderen.com.

Literature

Alcoholics Anonymous (AA). (1993). *Alcoholics Anonymous: The Story of How Many Thousands of Men and Women Have Recovered From Alcoholism*. New York: Alcoholics Anonymous World Services.
Black, C. (1981). *It Will Never Happen to Me: Growing Up With Addiction As Youngsters, Adolescents, Adults*. Center City, MN: Hazelden.
Carnes, P. (2012). *A Gentle Path Through the Twelve Steps: The Classic Guide for All People in the Process of Recovery*. Center City, MN: Hazelden.
Dunnington, K. (2011). *Addiction and Virtue: Beyond the Models of Disease and Choice*. Downers Grove, IL: IVP Academic.

Apologetics (Christian)

Literature

Bahnsen, G. L. (1998). *Van Til's Apologetic: Readings and Analysis*. Phillipsburg, NJ: P&R.
Groothuis, D. R. (2011). *Christian Apologetics: A Comprehensive Case for Biblical Faith*. Downers Grove, IL: IVP Academic.

On the Reliability of Biblical Text

Blomberg, C. L., & Stewart, R. B. (Eds.). (2016). *The Historical Reliability of the New Testament: Countering the Challenges to Evangelical Christian Beliefs*. Nashville, TN: B&H Academic.
Bruce, F. F. (2017). *New Testament Documents: Are They Reliable?* Grand Rapids: Eerdmans; Downers Grove, IL: InterVarsity.
Kaiser, W. C. (2001). *The Old Testament Documents: Are They Reliable & Relevant?* Downers Grove, IL: InterVarsity.

On the Problem of Evil

Clark, G. (1995). *Religion, Reason & Revelation* (pp. 194–242). Nobbs, NM: Trinity Foundation. (Original work published 1961)
Wright, R. K. M. (1996). *No Place for Sovereignty: What's Wrong With Freewill Theism* (pp. 177–203). Downers Grove, IL: InterVarsity.

For an Overview and Brief Critiques of Opinions on the Problem of Evil

Meister, C. V. & Dew, James K., Jr. (Eds.). (2017). *God and the Problem of Evil: Five Views*. Downers Grove, IL: IVP Academic.
Newport, J. P. (1989). *Life's Ultimate Questions: A Contemporary Philosophy of Religion* (pp. 217–55). Dallas: Word.

Attachment

General Information

Bowlby, J. (1969). *Attachment: Vol. 1. Attachment and Loss* New York: Basic.
Bowlby, J. (1972). *Separation: Anxiety and Anger: Vol. 2. Attachment and Loss*. London, UK: Hogarth.
Bowlby, J. (1980). *Loss, Sadness, and Depression: Vol. 3. Attachment and Loss*. London, UK: Hogarth.

Bowlby, J. (1982). Attachment and loss: Retrospect and prospect. *American Journal of Orthopsychiatry,* 52(4), 664–78. doi:https://doi.org/10.1111/j.1939-025.1982.tb01456

God as Attachment Figure

Boccia, M. L. (2011). Human Interpersonal Relationship and the Love of the Trinity. *Priscilla Papers,* 25(4), 22–26.
Kirkpatrick, L. A. (2005). *Attachment, Evolution, and the Psychology of Religion* (pp. 52–74). New York. Guilford.

Emotion-Focused Therapy (EFT) Theory and Practice

Johnson, S. M. (2004). *The Practice of Emotionally Focused Couple Therapy: Creating Connection.* New York: Brunner-Routledge.
Johnson, S. M. (2008). *Hold Me Tight: Seven Conversations for a Lifetime of Love.* New York: Little Brown.
Johnson, S. M. (2019). *Attachment Theory in Practice: Emotionally Focused Therapy (EFT) With Individuals, Couples and Families.* New York: Guilford.
EFT. www.iceeft.com.
Research supporting EFT. www.iceeft.com/eft-research.

Cognitive Skills (Building Reason, Logic, and Clarity)

Hurley, P. J., DeMarco, J. P., & Hurley, P. J. (2012). *Learning Logic 6.0: For Hurley's A Concise Introduction to Logic* (11th ed.). Belmont, CA: Wadsworth.
Pine, R. C. (1996). *Essential Logic: Basic Reasoning Skills for the Twenty-first Century.* New York: Oxford University Press.
Sire, J., (2000) *Habits of the Mind: Intellectual Life As a Christian Calling.* Downers Grove, IL: InterVarsity.

Cultic Studies Organizations

Secular

Cult Education Institute: https://www.culteducation.com; an educational, nonprofit Internet archive of information about religiously abusive groups and movements. The Executive Director is author and thought-reform consultant (interventionist) Rick A. Ross.
Freedom of Mind: https://freedomofmind.com; provides education, consultation, and counseling resources for those seeking recovery from the influences of religious and relational abuse. The Founding Director is author Steve Hassan, MEd, LMHC, NCC.

Info-Cult: www.infosecte.org; a Canadian-based, nonprofit/charitable organization offering information and help with regard to groups, their ideology, and their functioning, and also interpersonal relationships within a context of religious abuse. The founder, Executive Director, and often court-appointed consultant on religious abuse is Michael Kropveld.

Information Network Focus on Religious Movements (INFORM): https://inform.ac; an independent educational charity that provides up-to-date academic publications, seminars, events, research, and information about minority religions. The honorary acting director and prolific author is Sociology Professor Emeritus at the London School of Economics, Eileen Barker, PhD, OBE, FBA.

International Cultic Studies Association (ICSA): www.icsahome.com; a large and influential 501(c)(3) nonprofit, educational organization that provides practical, religious abuse-related resources and services for families, former group members, mental health professionals, clergy, attorneys, educators, and young people. ICSA membership primarily comprises professional clinicians, social workers, educators, researchers, thought-reform consultants, and a broad mix of others previously affected by undue influence or mind control. The President is Steven Eichel, PhD, ABPP and the longtime Executive Director and author is psychologist Michael Langone, PhD.

Christian

Apologetics Index: http://www.apologeticsindex.org; a widely respected, vast clearing house of religious-abuse news, information, and resources. The Executive Director is David Anderson.

Becoming Free, LLC: www.becomingfree.org; an organization that provides cultic-studies education, related support groups, life coaching, and conference speakers. The Executive Directors are author Patrick J. Knapp, PhD, and Heidi I. Knapp.

Center for Studies on New Religions (CESNUR): https://www.cesnur.org; an international network of associations of scholars working in cultic studies who provide information about abusive religious groups. The founder and Managing Director, Italian sociologist, and prolific author is Massimo Introvigne, JurD.

Christian Research Institute (CRI): www.equip.org; the largest and longest-operating nonprofit evangelical organization committed to Christian apologetics, and defense of the Christian faith, education on various religiously abusive groups; it also provides critiques of cultural concerns (abortion rights, euthanasia, etc.). CRI publishes an influential Christian Research Journal six times/year and provides a daily radio program, the *Bible Answer Man*. The Executive Director is author Hank Hanegraaff.

Darkness to Light (DTL): www.dtl.org; a large and broad informational website that provides thoughtful and carefully researched material on religious abuse, non-Christian beliefs, and critiques on cultural concerns. The founder, Executive Director, and author of several books is Gary Zeolla.

Evangelical Ministries to New Religions (EMNR): http://www.emnr.org; a nonprofit that provides educational events and information concerning religiously abusive groups and non-Christian beliefs. The Executive Director is Eric Pement MBA., MDiv.

MeadowHaven: http://www.meadowhaven.org/index.html; a medium-term (1-to-2 month) residential recovery center for those affected by religiously abusive environments. Most of MeadowHaven's work has been with former members of Bible-based abusive groups. The executive director is Bob Pardon, MDiv, ThM; the associate director is Judy Pardon, BA, MEd.

Reveal: http://www.reveal.org; an organization of former members of the International Churches of Christ (ICC; ICOC), Boston Church of Christ/ "Boston Movement," and Crossroads Church of Christ/"Crossroads Movement." This organization provides support for former members of these organizations and a list of similar support groups in the United States. The Executive Director is Chris Lee, MDiv.

Wellspring Retreat and Resource Center: https://wellspringretreat.org; currently being revamped. Wellspring was originally founded in 1986 by psychologist Dr. Paul Martin as a short-term (2-to-4 week) residential treatment center for those who have been religiously abused. Following Dr. Martin's death, Wellspring is now a counseling center located in Albany, Ohio that specializes in recovery from religious abuse. The Executive Director is Gregory Sammons, LPC.

Witnesses for Jesus: https://www.witnessesforjesus.org; an 501(c)(3) evangelical, parachurch, countercult educational ministry. It seeks to inform the public about the spiritual and sociological dangers of the Jehovah's Witnesses and Mormon religions. Along with providing written and web-based materials, the organization offers training in better understanding the Christian faith. It is located in Colorado Springs, Colorado, and the Executive Director is Christy Darlington.

Family Systems

Organizations

The Bowen Center. www.thebowencenter.org.
The Gottman Institute. www.gottman.com.

Theory Formulation

Kerr, M. E., & Bowen, M. (1988). *Family Evaluation: An Approach Based on Bowen Theory.* New York: Norton.

Minuchin, S., Nichols, M. P., & Lee, W.-Y. (2007). *Assessing Families and Couples: From Symptom to System.* Boston: Pearson/Allyn & Bacon.

Nichols, M. P., & Schwartz, R. C. (2010). *Family Therapy: Concepts and Methods.* Upper Saddle River, NJ: Pearson Education.

Walsh, F. (2003). *Normal Family Processes: Growing Diversity and Complexity.* New York: Guilford.

Applied to Relational Abuse

Cloud, H., & Cloud, H. (2011). *Unlocking Your Family Patterns: Finding Freedom From a Hurtful Past*. Chicago: Moody.

VanVonderen, J. (2010). *Families Where Grace Is in Place: Building a Home Free of Manipulation, Legalism, and Shame*. Minneapolis, MN: Bethany. (Original work published 1992)

Applied to Religious Institutions

Aguado, J. (2018). "How a Dysfunctional Family Functions Like a Cult." *ICSA Today*, 9(3), 2–7. Retrieved from https://www.icsahome.com/articles/how-a-dysfunctional-family-functions-like-a-cult.

Ducklow, P. & Ducklow, C. (n.d.). "Understanding Family Process in Church Life: Utilizing the Skills of Family Systems Theory in Church Leadership." Unpublished. Retrieved from http://www.theducklows.ca/frames/tools/articles/FamilyProcessAndChurchLife.pdf.

Friedman, E. H. (1985). *Generation to Generation: Family Process in Church and Synagogue*. New York: Guilford.

Empirical Research

Goldenberg, E., Stanton, M., & Goldenberg, H. (2017). *Family Therapy: An Overview* (pp. 416–42). Boston: Cengage Learning.

Gottman, J. M., & Schwartz, J. G. (2018). *The Science of Couples and Family Therapy: Behind the Scenes at the Love Lab* (pp. 63–67). New York: Norton.

Hermeneutics

Chrnalogar, M. A. (2000). *Twisted Scriptures: Breaking Free From Churches That Abuse*. Grand Rapids, MI: Zondervan.

Klein, W. W., Blomberg, C. L., & Hubbard, R. L. (2017). *Introduction to Biblical Interpretation*. Grand Rapids, MI: Zondervan.

Sire, J. (1980). *Scripture Twisting: Twenty Ways the Cults Misread the Bible*. Downers Grove, IL: InterVarsity.

Marriage

General Growth and Development

Gottman, J., & Silver, N. (2015). *The Seven Principles for Making Marriage Work: A Practical Guide From the Country's Foremost Relationship Expert*. New York: Harmony.

Johnson, S., & Sanderfer, K. (2016). *Created for Connection: The "Hold Me Tight" Guide for Christian Couples*. New York: Little, Brown Spark.

Yerkovich, M., & Yerkovich, K. (2008). *How We Love: Discover Your Love Style, Enhance Your Marriage*. Colorado Springs, CO: Waterbrook. (Original work published 2006)

Research Source on the Broad Topic of Marriage

The Gottman Institute. www.gottman.com/about/research.

Gender Roles

Balswick, J. O., & Balswick, J. K. (2011). *The Family: A Christian Perspective on the Contemporary Home* (pp. 187–236).Grand Rapids, MI: Baker Academic.

Christian for Biblical Equality (CBE) egalitarian website. www.cbe.org.

Groothuis, R. M. (1994). *Women Caught in the Conflict: The Culture War Between Traditionalism and Feminism*. Grand Rapids, MI: Baker.

Pierce, R. W. (2010). *Discovering Biblical Equality: Complementarity without Hierarchy*. Downers Grove, IL: InterVarsity.

Pastoral

Understanding Family Systems Theory

Ducklow, P., & Ducklow, C. (n.d.). *Family Systems Theory, Theology and Thought*. Unpublished. Retrieved from http://www.theducklows.ca/frames/tools/articles/FamilySystemsTheoryTheologyAndThought.pdf.

Leadership

Barrs, J. (1983). *Shepherds & Sheep: A Biblical View of Leading & Following*. Downers Grove, IL: InterVarsity.

Powers, H. (2018). *Redemptive Leadership: Unleashing Your Greatest Influence*. Littleton, CO: Illumify Media Global.

Tillapaugh, F. R. (1982). *The Church Unleashed*. Ventura, CA: Regal.

Spiritual Development

Schaeffer, F. A. (2001) *True Spirituality*. Wheaton, IL: Tyndale. (Original work published 1971)

Thomas, G. (2010). *Sacred Pathways: Discover Your Soul's Path to God*. Grand Rapids, MI: Zondervan.

VanVonderen, J., Ryan, D., & Ryan, J. (2008). *Soul Repair: Rebuilding Your Spiritual Life.* Downers Grove, IL: InterVarsity.

Webster, D. D. (1999). *Soulcraft: How God Shapes Us Through Relationships.* Downers Grove, IL: InterVarsity.

Safe-Haven Formation

Damgaard, N. (2015). A safe-haven church: An introduction to the basics of a safe religious community. *ICSA Today,* 6(1), 2–7.

Cultural Influences Upon the Church

Dawn, M. (1995). *Reaching Out Without Dumbing Down: A Theology of Worship for the Turn-of-the-Century Culture.* Grand Rapids, MI: Eerdmans.

Groothuis, D. (2001). *Truth Decay: Defending Christianity Against the Challenges of Postmodernism.* Downers Grove, IL: InterVarsity.

Webster, D. D. (2009). *Selling Jesus: What's Wrong With Marketing the Church.* Eugene, OR: Wipf & Stock.

General Website for Pastoral Resources on Recovery From Religious Abuse

Spiritual Abuse Resources. https://www.spiritualabuseresources.com/spiritual-safe-haven-network

Redemptive Stories

General Historic Examples

John Newton (author of hymn, *Amazing Grace*). www.monergism.com/benefits-affliction.

Joni Erickson Tada (quadriplegic due to injury). www.joniearecksontadastory.com.

Nick Vujicic (congenital absence of limbs). http://www.nickvujicic.com.

Appendix C
Religious Abuse Biographies/Autobiographies

Duncan, W. J. (2006). *I Can't Hear God Anymore: Life in a Dallas Cult*. Garland, TX: VN Life Resources.

Hutchinson, J. (1994). *Out of the Cults and Into the Church: Understanding & Encouraging Ex-Cultists*. Grand Rapids, MI: Kregel Resources.

Knapp, P. (1998). "Nothing Need Go to Waste," *Cultic Studies Journal*, 5(2), 120–29. Retrieved from https://docs.wixstatic.com/ugd/79a2a8_8c018ab466144099a045d7 e0a21aecff.pdf.

Metaxas, E. (2017). *Martin Luther: The Man Who Rediscovered God and Changed the World*. New York: Viking.

Redemptive Biblical Stories

Noah (Gen 6–8)
Joseph (Gen 32–50)
Ruth (Ruth 1–4)
Lost Sheep (Luke 15:1–7)
Prodigal Son (Luke 15:11–32)

Support Groups

Literature

Goldberg, W. "Overview: Support Groups" (pp. 261–62); Goldberg, W. & Goldberg, L. "Support Group for Former Cult Members" (pp. 265–75); Knapp, P. J. "An Independent Faith-Based Approach to Support and Recovery Groups for Those Affected by Harmful Religious Environments" (pp. 261–97). In Goldberg, L., Goldberg W., Henry, R., & Langone, M. (Eds.). (2017). *Cult Recovery: A Clinician's Guild to Working With Former Members and Families*. Bonita Springs, FL: ICSA.

Websites

Becoming Free, LLC. https://www.becomingfree.org/support-recovery-groups.

ICSA-identified Sources. https://docs.google.com/document/d/1uLOlc5Hz6VAnvROsN 43CSZq29MwuJCQkyfIVaJEcmTo/edit.

Psychcentral. https://psychcentral.com/resources/Abuse/Support Groups.

Spiritual Abuse. http://www.spiritualabuse.org/ck/supportgroup.html.

Survivors Network of Those Abused by Priests (SNAP). http://www.snapnetwork.org.

Theology (Christian)

Systematic Theology Literature

Erickson, M. J. (2013). *Christian Theology*. Grand Rapids, MI: Baker Academic.

Grudem, W. (2007). *Systematic Theology: An Introduction to Biblical Doctrine*. Leicester, UK: InterVarsity. (Original work published 1997)

Lewis, G. R., & Demarest, B. A. (2014). *Integrative Theology*.Grand Rapids, MI: Zondervan.

Pastoral Authority

Barrs, J. (1983). *Shepherds & Sheep: A Biblical View of Leading & Following*. Downers Grove, IL: InterVarsity.

Enroth, R. (1979). "The Power Abusers: When Follow-the-Leader Becomes a Dangerous Game." *Eternity*. Retrieved from www.apologeticsindex.org/a08.html.

Macaulay, R., & Barrs, J. (1978). *Being Human: The Nature of Spiritual Experience* (see comments regarding the theology of Watchman Nee, pp. 45, 51–52, 78, 200n8, 203nn20–24, 204nn1, 5). Downers Grove, IL: IVP Academic.

Watchman Nee theological critiques.

> http://www.dtl.org/cults/review/authority.html.
> http://www.apologeticsindex.org/2694-watching-out-for-watchman-nee.
> https://www.douglasjacoby.com/watchman-nee-on-soul-spirit-by-gordon-ferguson.

Spirituality

Johnson, A. L. (1988). *Faith Misguided: Exposing the Dangers of Mysticism*. Chicago: Moody.

Macaulay, R., & Barrs, J. (1998). *Being Human: The Nature of Spiritual Experience*. Downers Grove, IL: IVP Academic.

Schaeffer, F. A. (2011). *True Spirituality*. Carol Stream, IL: Tyndale. (Original work published 1971)

Human Will and Responsibility

Clark, G. H. (1995). *Religion, Reason, and Revelation* (pp. 220–222). Philadelphia: Presbyterian and Reformed. (Original work published 1961)

Wright, R. K. M. (1996). *No Place for Sovereignty: What's Wrong With Freewill Theism* (pp. 43–62). Downers Grove, IL: InterVarsity.

Appendix C
Thought Reform Consultants (Interventionists)

Joseph Kelly (joekelly411@gmail.com). www.intervention101.com.
Patrick Ryan (cultnews101@googlegroups.com). www.intervention101.com.
Steven Hassan (center@freedomofmind.com). https://freedomofmind.com.
Rick Ross (info@culteducation.com). https://www.culteducation.com/prep_faq.html.
David Clark (cultspecs2@comcast.net).

Trauma Recovery

Herman, J. L. (2015). *Trauma and Recovery: Aftermath of Violence From Domestic Abuse to Political Terror.* New York: Basic. (Original work published 1997)

Kolk, B. van der (2015). *The Body Keeps the Score: Brain, Mind and Body in the Healing of Trauma.* New York: Penguin.

Kolk, B. van der, McFarlane, A., & Weisaeth, L. (Eds.). (2007). *Traumatic Stress: The Effects of Overwhelming Experience on Mind, Body, and Society.* New York: Guilford. (Original work published 1996)

References

Ackerman, C. (2017, Oct.) *Emotion focused therapy: Understanding emotions to improve relationships.* (PositivePsychologyProgram blog.) Available online at https://positivepsychologyprogram.com/emotion-focused-therapy/

Aguado, J. (2018). How a dysfunctional family functions like a cult. *ICSA Today, 9*(3), 2–7. Available online at https://www.icsahome.com/articles/how-a-dysfunctional-family-functions-like-a-cult

Ainsworth, M. D. S. (1967). *Infancy in Uganda: Infant care and the growth of love.* Baltimore, MD: Johns Hopkins Press.

A.A. World Services. (2001). *Alcoholics Anonymous* (4th ed.). New York, NY: author.

Al Fadi, Mutee'a (n.d.). *The dilemma of Jihad doctrine: The myth of Quranic warnings vs. violence commands* [posted on Answering Islam site]. Retrieved from http://www.answering-islam.org/authors/alfadi/jihad.html

American Psychological Association. (1987, May). Board of Social and Ethical Responsibility for Psychology (memo to the DIMPAC Committee). Washington, DC: American Psychological Association.

Armstrong, K. (2014/2015). *Fields of blood: Religion and the history of violence.* (Originally published in 2014). New York, NY:Anchor Books.

Arterburn, S., & Felton, J. (1991). *Toxic faith: Understanding and overcoming religious addiction.* Nashville, TN: Oliver Nelson.

Asbridge, T. (2010). *The Crusades: The authoritative history of the war for the Holy Land.* New York, NY: Ecco/HarperCollins.

Ash, S. M. (1983). *Cult induced psychopathology: A critical review of presuppositions, conversion, clinical picture, and treatment.* (Doctoral dissertation). Rosemead College, CA.

Audi, R. (2001). *The Cambridge dictionary of philosophy.* Cambridge, MA: Cambridge University Press.

Baloian, B. E. (1992). *Anger in the Old Testament.* New York, NY: P. Lang.

Barker, E. (1984). *The Making of a Moonie: Choice or brainwashing?* Oxford, UK: Blackwell.

———. (1995). *New religious movements: A practical introduction.* (Originally published in 1989.) London, UK: HMSO.

Bauer, W., Arndt, W. F., and Gingrich, F. W. (1957). *A Greek-English lexicon of the New Testament and other early Christian literature.* From German 4th revised and augmented edition. Chicago: University of Chicago.

Beck, J. S. (2011). *Cognitive therapy: Basics and beyond.* New York, NY: Guilford Press.

References

Bertalanffy, L. V. (1968). *General system theory: foundations, development, applications.* New York, NY: Braziller.

Black, C. (1981). *It will never happen to me.* Denver, CO: MAC Publishing.

Boccia, M. (2011). Human interpersonal relationships and the love of the trinity. *Priscilla Papers, Vol. 25, No. 4* (Autumn), 22–26. Available online at https://www.cbeinternational.org/sites/default/files/Human_Boccia.pdf

Booth, L. (1991). *When God becomes a drug: Breaking the chains of religious addiction & abuse.* Los Angeles, CA: J.P. Tarcher.

Bowlby, J. (1969). *Attachment (Attachment and loss, vol. 1).* Harmondsworth, UK: Penguin.

———. (1972). *Separation: Anxiety and anger (Attachment and loss, vol. 2).* London, UK: Hogarth Press.

———. (1980). *Loss, sadness and depression (Attachment and loss, vol. 3).* London, UK: Hogarth Press.

———. (1982, October). Attachment and loss: Retrospect and prospect. *American Journal of Orthopsychiatry, 52*(4), 664–78. doi:https://doi.org/10.1111/j.1939-025.1982.tb01456.x

Breault, M., & King, M. (1993). *Inside the cult: A member's chilling, exclusive account of madness and depravity in David Koresh's compound.* London, UK: Signet/Penguin.

Bromley, D. G., & Hammond, P. E. (Eds.). (1987). *The future of new religious movements.* New Ecumenical Research Association (Unification Theological Seminary). Macon, GA: Mercer University Press.

Bromley, D. G., & Melton, J. G. (2002). *Cults, religion, and violence.* New York, NY: Cambridge University Press.

Bromley, D. G., & Shupe, A. D. (1981). *Strange gods: The great American cult scare.* Boston, MA: Beacon Press.

Brown, C. (1990). *Christianity & Western thought: A history of philosophers, ideas & movements.* Downers Grove, Ill: InterVarsity Press.

Bunyan, J. (2016). *Pilgrim's progress.* (Originally published in 1675.) Carol Stream, IL: Tyndale House.

Bunyan, J., Beaumont, A., & Furlong, M. (1978). *The trial of John Bunyan & the persecution of the Puritans: Selections from the writings of John Bunyan and Agnes Beaumont.* London, UK: Folio Society.

Challies, T. (2014). The false teachers: Pelagius. (Feb. 23 blog). available online at https://www.challies.com/articles/the-false-teachers-pelagius/

Christian Research Institute (CRI). (2009, April 14). CRI Statement, Article ID: DD025 available at: https://www.equip.org/article/the-branch-davidians/

Chrnalogar, M. A. (2000). *Twisted scriptures: Breaking free from churches that abuse.* Grand Rapids, MI: Zondervan

Churchill, Winston, Sir. (1942). *The end of the beginning* (speech at London's Mansion House). Available online at http://www.churchill-society-london.org.uk/EndoBegn.html

Clark, D. (1998). Bible cult mind control 101. *Cultic Studies Journal, 15*(2), 139–50.

Clark, D. K. (1993). *Dialogical apologetics: A person-centered approach to Christian defense. Grand Rapids,* MI: Baker Books.

Clark, G. H. (1995). *Religion, reason, and revelation.* (Originally published in 1961.) Hobbs, NM: Trinity Foundation.

References

Cloud, H., & Townsend, J. S. (2008). *Boundaries in marriage: An 8-session focus on understanding the boundaries that make or break loving relationships.* Place of publication not identified: Zondervan.

Conway, F., & Siegelman, J. (1995). *Snapping: America's epidemic of sudden personality change.* New York, NY: Stillpoint Press.

Cooper, B., Cox, D., Lienesch, R., & Jones, R. P. (2016). *Exodus: Why Americans are leaving religion—And why they're unlikely to come back.* Public Religion Research Institute (PRRI). Retrieved from https://www.prri.org/research/prri-rns-poll-nones-atheist-leaving-religion/

Cowan, D. E., & Bromley, D. G. (2008). *Cults and new religions: A brief history.* Malden, MA: Blackwell.

Christian Research Institute (CRI). (2009, April). *The Branch Davidians.* Article ID DD025. Available online at https://www.equip.org/article/the-branch-davidians/

Damgaard, N. (2015). A safe-haven church: An introduction to the basics of a safe religious community. *ICSA Today, Vol. 6, No.1,* 2–7.

David, D., Cristea, I., & Hofmann, S. G. (2018). Why cognitive behavioral therapy is the current gold standard of psychotherapy. *Frontiers in Psychiatry, 9*(4). Also available online at https://www.ncbi.nlm.nih.gov/pmc/articles/PMC5797481/

Dawkins, R. (2006). *The God delusion.* Boston MA; New York, NY: Houghton Mifflin.

Dennett, D. C. (2006). *Breaking the spell: Religion as a natural phenomenon.* New York, NY: Penguin Books.

Dennis, E. S. G., Jr. (1993). *Evaluation of the handling of the Branch Davidian stand-off in Waco, Texas : February 28 to April 19, 1993.* United States Department of Justice. Washington, DC: US Government Printing Office.

Dinneen, M. (2013). *The gift of fulfillment: Living the principles of healthy recovery.* Las Vegas, NV: Central Recovery Press.

Duncan, W. J. (2006). *I can't hear God anymore: Life in a Dallas cult.* Rowlett, TX: VM Life Resources.

Dunnington, K. (2011). *Addiction and virtue: Beyond the models of disease and choice.* Downers Grove, IL: IVP Academic.

Edwards, J. (1746). *A treatise concerning religious affections, in three parts.* Boston, MA: S. Kneeland and T. Green.

Edwards, J., & Houston, J. M. (1996). *Religious affections: A Christian's character before God.* (Originally published in 1744.) Minneapolis, MN: Bethany House.

Edwards, J., Ramsay, P., Smith, J. E., & Goen, C. C. (2009). *The works of Jonathan Edwards.* New Haven, CT: Yale University Press.

Elliott, M. (2006). *Faithful feelings: Rethinking emotion in the New Testament.* Grand Rapids, MI: Kregel.

Engh, M. J. (2007). *In the name of heaven: 3,000 years of religious persecution.* Amherst, NY: Prometheus Books.

Enroth, R. M. (1992). *Churches that abuse.* Grand Rapids, MI: Zondervan.

———. (1994). *Recovery from churches that abuse.* Grand Rapids, MI: Zondervan.

Enroth, R. M., & Melton, J. G. (1985). *Why cults succeed where the church fails.* Elgin, IL: Brethren Press.

Erickson, M. J. (1998). *Christian theology.* Grand Rapids, MI: Baker Book.

Farley, W. P. (2006.) Charles Finney: The controversial evangelist. *Enrichment Journal.* Available online at http://enrichmentjournal.ag.org/200601/200601_118_Finney.cfm

References

Ford, C. V., & Bunyan, J. (1675/2016). *The pilgrim's progress discipleship course: A companion study to Bunyan's the pilgrim's progress.* Bloomington, IN: WestBowPress.

Foxe, J., & Wright, P. (1811). *The new and complete book of martyrs; or, an universal history of martyrdom: Being Fox's book of martyrs, revised and corrected, with additions and great improvements.* London, UK: Hogg.

Frankl, V. E. (1984). *Man's search for meaning, revised and updated.* (Originally published in German in 1946 as *Trotzdem Ja zum Leben sagen: Ein Psychologe erlebt das Konzentrationslager* [*In spite of all* [*that happened*] *say yes to life: A psychologist experiences the concentration camp*].) New York, NY: Washington Square.

————. (1997/2011). *Man's search for ultimate meaning.* London, UK: Rider.

Frend, W. H. C. (1981). *Martyrdom and persecution in the early church: A study of a conflict from the Maccabees to Donatus.* Grand Rapids, MI: Baker Book House.

————. (1986). *The rise of Christianity.* London, UK: Darton, Longman & Todd.

Friedman, E. H. (1985). *Generation to generation: Family process in church and synagogue.* New York, NY: Guilford Press.

Galanter, M. (Ed.). (1989). *Cults and new religious movements: A report of the American Psychiatric Association* (from the Committee on Psychiatry and Religion). Washington, DC: American Psychiatric Association.

Galindo, I., Boomer, E., & Reagan, D. (2006). *A family genogram workbook.* Richmond, VA: Educational Consultants.

Giambalvo, C., & Rosedale, H. L. (1996). *The Boston Movement: Critical perspectives on the International Churches of Christ.* Bonita Springs, FL: American Family Foundation.

Goldberg, L. (1993). Chapter 11: Guidelines for therapists. In Langone, M. D., *Recovery from cults: Help for victims of psychological and spiritual abuse* (pp. 232–50). New York, NY: W.W. Norton.

————. (2017a). Overview: Helping former members—Individual psychotherapy. In Goldberg, L., Goldberg, W., Henry, R., & Langone, M. (Eds.). (2017). *Cult recovery: A clinician's guide to working with former members and families* (pp. 55–67). Bonita Springs, FL: ICSA.

————. (2017b). Chapter 11: Helping first-generation parents and second-generation children heal the impact of cult harm. In Goldberg, L., Goldberg, W., Henry, R., & Langone, M. (Eds.). (2017). *Cult recovery: A clinician's guide to working with former members and families* (pp. 241–58). Bonita Springs, FL: ICSA.

Goldberg, L. & Goldberg, W. (2017). Chapter 12: Support group for former cult members. In Goldberg, L., Goldberg, W., Henry, R., & Langone, M. (Eds.). (2017). *Cult recovery: A clinician's guide to working with former members and families* (pp. 265–75). Bonita Springs, FL: ICSA.

Goldberg, L., Goldberg, W., Henry, R., & Langone, M. (Eds.). (2017). *Cult recovery: A clinician's guide to working with former members and families.* Bonita Springs, FL: ICSA.

Goldberg, W. (1993). Guidelines for support groups. In M. Langone (Ed.), *Recovery from cults: Help for victims of psychological and spiritual abuse* (pp 275–84). New York, NY: W.W. Norton.

————. (2017a). Overview: Helping families and loved ones. In Goldberg, L., Goldberg, W., Henry, R., & Langone, M. (Eds.). (2017). *Cult recovery: A clinician's guide to working with former members and families* (p. 3–5). Bonita Springs, FL: ICSA.

———. (2017b). Chapter 1: Working with families. In Goldberg, L., Goldberg, W., Henry, R., & Langone, M. (Eds.). (2017). *Cult recovery: A clinician's guide to working with former members and families* (p. 7–17). Bonita Springs, FL: ICSA.

———. (2017c). Overview: Support groups. In Goldberg, L., Goldberg, W., Henry, R., & Langone, M. (Eds.). (2017). *Cult recovery: A clinician's guide to working with former members and families* (pp. 261–62). Bonita Springs, FL: ICSA.

Greenberg, L. (2004). *Process experiential psychotherapy: An emotion-focused approach.* (DVD). Washington, DC: American Psychological Association.

Gritsch, E. W. (2012). *Martin Luther's anti-Semitism: Against his better judgment.* Grand Rapids, MI. Eerdmans.

Groothuis, D. (2000). *Truth decay: Defending Christianity against the challenges of postmodernism.* Downers Grove, IL: IVP.

———. (2011). *Christian apologetics: A comprehensive case for biblical faith.* Downers Grove, IL: IVP Academic.

Hanegraaff, H. (2001). *Counterfeit revival.* Nashville, TN: Word Publishing.

———. (2012). *Christianity in crisis: The 21st century.* [Place of publication not identified]: Thomas Nelson.

Hargrove, B. (1989). *The sociology of religion: Classical and contemporary approaches* (2nd ed.). Arlington Heights, IL: Harlan Davidson.

Hassan, S. (2000). *Releasing the bonds: Empowering people to think for themselves.* Somerville, MA: Freedom of Mind Press.

———. (2012). *Freedom of mind: Helping loved ones leave controlling people, cults and beliefs.* Newton MA: Freedom of Mind Press.

———. (2015). *Combating cult mind control: The #1 best-selling guide to protection, rescue, and recovery from destructive cults.* (First published in 1988.) Newton MA: Freedom of Mind Press.

———. (2016, Sept. 16). *Robert Jay Lifton MD: An interview with a genius* [interview]. Available online from https://freedomofmind.com/robert-jay-lifton-m-d-an-interview-with-a-genius/

Hatch, N. O. (1989). *The democratization of American Christianity.* New Haven, CT: Yale University Press.

Hazler, R. J. (2016). Person-centered theory. In D. Capuzzi & M. D. Stauffer (Eds.), *Counseling and psychotherapy theories and interventions,* 6th ed. (pp. 169–93). Alexandria, VA: American Counseling Association.

Henry, R. (2017). Mentalization attachment approach to cult recovery. In L. Goldberg, W. Goldberg, R. Henry, & M. Langone (Eds.), *Cult recovery: A clinician's guide to working with former members and families* (pp. 117–38). Bonita Springs, FL: ICSA.

Herman, J. L. (1997/2015). *Trauma and recovery.* New York, NY: BasicBooks.

Hexam, I., & Poewe, K. O. (2000). *Understanding cults and new age religions.* Vancouver, BC: Regent College Publishing.

Houssney, G. (2010). *Engaging Islam,* Boulder, CO: Treeline Publishing.

Hutchinson, J. (1994). *Out of the cults and into the church: Understanding & encouraging ex-cultists.* Grand Rapids, MI: Kregel Resources.

Jenkinson, G. (2017). Chapter 16: Relational psychoeducational intensive: Time away for postcult counseling. In L. Goldberg, W. Goldberg, R. Henry, & M. Langone (Eds.), *Cult recovery: A clinician's guide to working with former members and families* (pp. 339–65). Bonita Springs, FL: ICSA.

Johnson, A. L. (1988). *Faith misguided: Exposing the dangers of mysticism.* Chicago, IL: Moody Press.

Johnson, D., & Allen, T. (1998). *Joy comes in the mourning—And other blessings in disguise: The beatitudes in action.* Camp Hill, PA: Christian Publications.

Johnson, D., & VanVonderen, J. (1991). *The subtle power of spiritual abuse: Recognizing & escaping spiritual manipulation and false spiritual authority.* Minneapolis, MN: Bethany House.

Johnson, P. (1976). *A history of Christianity.* New York, NY: Simon & Schuster.

———. (1997). *A history of the American people.* New York, NY: HarperCollins.

Johnson, S. M. (2008). *Hold me tight: Seven conversations for a lifetime of love.* New York, NY: Little, Brown.

———. (2019). *Attachment theory in practice: Emotionally focused therapy (EFT) with individuals, couples, and families.* New York, NY: Gilford Press.

Johnson, S., & Sanderfer, K. (2016). *Created for connection: the "hold me tight" guide for Christian couples.* New York, NY: Little Brown Spark.

Josephus, F., & W. Whiston (2003). *The complete works of Flavius Josephus.* Nashville, TN: T. Nelson.

Keller, T. (2014, April 29). Everything sad . . . [Timothy Keller, tweet]. Available online at https://twitter.com/timkellernyc/status/461143119170646018?lang=en

Kerns, K. A., Matthews, B. L., Koehn, A. J., Williams, C. T., & Siener-Ciesla, S. (2015). Assessing both safe haven and secure base support in parent-child relationships. *Attachment and Human Development 17*(4), 337–53.

Kilduff, M., & Javers, R. (1978). *The suicide cult: The inside story of the Peoples Temple sect and the massacre in Guyana.* New York: Bantam Books.

Kimble, M. (2000). *Viktor Frankl's contribution to spirituality and aging.* New York, NY:

Kirkpatrick, L. A. (2005). *Attachment, evolution and the psychology of religion.* New York, NY: Gilford Press.

Knapp, H. (2018). *Marriage issues for the spiritually abused.* Presentation at ISCA's Recovery From Spiritual Abuse conference, Hartford, CT, Oct. 26–27, 2018.

Knapp, P. (n.d.). About Becoming Free LLC. Retrieved from www.BecomingFree.org

———. (1998). Nothing need go to waste. *Cultic Studies Journal, 15*(2), 120–29.

———. (2000). *The place of mind control in the cult recovery process.* (Master's thesis, Denver Seminary, CO.)

———. (2017). Chapter 13: An independent faith-based approach to support and recovery groups for those affected by harmful religious environments. In L. Goldberg, W. Goldberg, R. Henry, & M. Langone, *Cult recovery: A clinician's guide to working with former members and families* (pp. 277–97). Bonita Springs, FL: ICSA.

Kurian, G. T., & Smith, J. D. (2010). *The encyclopedia of Christian literature: Volume 2.* Lanham, MD: Scarecrow Press.

Lalich, J. (1996, Spring). Repairing the soul after a cult. *CSNetwork Magazine,* 30–33.

———. (2004). *Bounded choice: True believers and charismatic cults.* Berkley, CA: University of California Press.

———. (n.d.). About Dr. Lalich. Cult Research & Information Center. Retrieved from http://cultresearch.org/about/

Lalich, J., & Tobias, M. L. (2006). *Take back your life: Recovering from cults and abusive relationships.* Berkeley, CA: Bay Tree Press.

Lalich, J., & McLaren K. (2018). *Escaping Utopia: Growing up in a cult, getting out, and starting over.* New York, NY: Routledge.

References

Langone, M. D. (n.d.). Overview: Researchers. Available online at http://www.icsahome.com/elibrary/studyguides/research

———. (1993). *Recovery from cults: Help for victims of psychological and spiritual abuse.* New York, NY: W.W. Norton.

———. (1995). Secular and religious critiques of cults: Complementary visions, not irresolvable conflicts. *Cultic Studies Journal, 12*(2), 166–86.

———. (1996, July). Clinical update on cults. *Psychiatric Times.* Retrieved from http://citeseerx.ist.psu.edu/viewdoc/download?doi=10.1.1.739.3546&rep=rep1&type=pdf

———. (2015). The definitional ambiguity of *cult* and ICSA's mission. *ICSA Today, 6*(3), 6–7.

———. (2017a). Introduction. In L. Goldberg, W. Goldberg, R. Henry, & M. Langone, *Cult recovery: A clinician's guide to working with former members and families* (pp. xvii–xxiii). Bonita Springs, FL: ICSA.

———. (2017b). Overview: Special issues and research, In L. Goldberg, W. Goldberg, R. Henry, & M. Langone, *Cult recovery: A clinician's guide to working with former members and families* (pp. 391–92). Bonita Springs, FL: ICSA.

Langone, M. D., & Chambers, W. (1991). Outreach to ex-cult members: The question of terminology. *Cultic Studies Journal,* 8(2). 134–50.

Laymon, B. (2018). *Spirituality in individuality and togetherness: A quantitative analysis based in Bowen theory.* (Doctoral dissertation, Loyola University, Maryland). Retrieved from file:///C:/Users/Pat/Downloads/LaymonDissertation2018.pdf

Layton, D. (1999). *Seductive poison: A Jonestown survivor's story of life and death in the Peoples Temple.* New York, NY: Anchor Books.

Lewis, C. S. (1946). *The great divorce.* London: Collins.

Lifton, R. J. (1961/1989). *Thought reform and the psychology of totalism: A study of "brainwashing" in China.* (Reprinted, with a new preface in 1989.) Chapel Hill, NC: University of North Carolina Press.

———. (1981, February). Cult formation. *The Harvard Mental Health Letter, Vol. 7, No. 8.*

———. (1987). *The future of immortality: And other essays for a nuclear age.* New York, NY: Basic Books.

Lindsey, L. (2014). *Recovering agency: Lifting the veil of Mormon mind control.* Place of publication not identified.

Lobdell, W. (2009). *Losing my religion: How I lost my faith reporting on religion in America.* New York, NY: HarperCollins.

Maalouf, A., & Rothschild, J. (2012). *The Crusades through Arab eyes.* London, UK: Saqi.

Macaulay, R., & Barrs, J. (1978). *Being human: The nature of spiritual experience.* Downers Grove, IL: InterVarsity Press.

MacCulloch, D. (2015) *The Reformation: A history.* New York, NY: Penguin.

Martin, P. (1987). Post-Cult. *Cultic Studies Journal,* 4.2/5.1, 59–121.

———. (1989, winter/spring). Dispelling the myths: The psychological consequences of cultic involvement. *Christian Research Journal, 11,* 9–14.

———. (1990). Post-cult rehabilitation counseling. *Wellspring Messenger, 1*(3), 1.

———. (1993a). Post-cult recovery: Assessment and rehabilitation. In M. L. Langone (Ed.), *Recovery from cults* (p. 203–32). New York, NY: W.W. Norton.

———. (1993b). Wellspring's approach to cult rehab. *Wellspring Messenger, 4*(5), 1.

———. (1993c). *Cult proofing your kids.* Grand Rapids, MI: Zondervan.

———. (1999). Toxic faith or thought reform. *Wellspring Messenger, 8*(2), 1–4, 19–23.

————. (2000). Toxic faith or thought reform, part 2. *Wellspring Messenger, 9*(1), 1–2, 15–20.

Martin, P., Pile, L., Burks, R., & Martin, S. (1998). Overcoming the bondage of revictimization: A rational/empirical defense of thought reform. *Cultic Studies Journal, 15*(2), 151–91.

Martin, W. (1977). *The kingdom of the cults.* (Originally published in 1965.) Minneapolis, MN: Bethany Fellowship.

————. (1980). *The new cults.* Ventura, CA: Regal Books.

————. (2003). *The kingdom of the cults: An analysis of the major cult systems in the present Christian era.* (Originally published in 1965). Minneapolis, MN: Bethany Fellowship.

Martin, W., & Hanegraaff, H. (Ed.). (1997). *The kingdom of the cults.* Minneapolis, MN: Bethany House.

Martin, W., & Zacharias, R. K. (2003). *The kingdom of the cults: The definitive work on the subject.* Minneapolis, MN: Bethany House.

Miner, M. H. (June 01, 2007). Back to the basics in attachment to God: Revisiting theory in light of theology. *Journal of Psychology and Theology, 35,* 2, 112–22.

Murray, I. (1994). Revival and revivalism. Edinburgh: Banner of Truth.

Nee, W. (1972). *Spiritual authority.* New York: Christian Fellowship Publishers.

Newport, J. P. (1989). *Life's ultimate questions: A contemporary philosophy of religion.* Dallas, TX: Word Publishing.

Newport, K. G. C. (2006). *The Branch Davidians of Waco: The history and beliefs of an apocalyptic sect.* Oxford, UK: Oxford University Press.

Newton, J. (1776). The benefits of affliction (from *The Letters of John Newton*). Available online at https://www.monergism.com/benefits-affliction

Noll, M. (1992). *A history of Christianity in the United States and Canada.* Grand Rapids, MI: Eerdmans.

Ofshe, R. (1992). "Coercive Persuasion and Attitude Change." In E. Borgatta & M. Borgatta (Eds.), *The Encyclopedia of Sociology, Vol. 1,* 212–24. New York, NY: Macmillan.

Orlowski, B. M. (2010). *Spiritual abuse recovery: Dynamic research on finding a place of wholeness.* Eugene, OR: Wipf & Stock.

Pardon, R., & Pardon, J. (2017). Chapter 17: Residential treatment modality for cult trauma survivors. In L. Goldberg, W. Goldberg, R. Henry, & M. Langone, *Cult recovery: A clinician's guide to working with former members and families* (pp. 367–89). Bonita Springs, FL: ICSA.

Passantino, B., & Passantino, G. (1994, Spring). Overcoming the bondage of victimization. *Cornerstone, 22*(102–3), 31–40.

————. (1997). Critiquing cult mind-control model. In W. Martin & H. Hanegraaff (Ed.), *The kingdom of the cults* (revised ed.; pp. 49–78). Minneapolis, MN: Bethany House.

Psychology Harassment Information Association. (n.d.). Margaret Singer/Margaret Thaler Singer, PhD biography. Available online at http://www.psychologicalharassment.com/Margaret-Thaler-Singer-Biography.htm

Reavis, D. J. (1995). *The ashes of Waco: An investigation.* New York, NY: Simon & Schuster.

Regina, W. F. (2011). *Applying family systems theory to mediation.* Lanham, MD: Univ. Press of America.

Reisz, S., Brennan, J., Jacobvitz, D., & George, C. (2019). Adult attachment and birth experience: Importance of a secure base and safe haven during childbirth. *Journal of Reproductive and Infant Psychology, 37*(1), 26–43.

References

The Religion of Peace.com (TROP). (n.d.). List of Islamic terror: 2016. Available online at https://www.thereligionofpeace.com/terror-2016.htm

Rhodes, R. (2013). *The challenge of the cults and new religions: The essential guide to their history, their doctrine, and our response.* Grand Rapids, MI: Zondervan.

Robbins, T., & Anthony, D. (1990). *In gods we trust: New patterns of religious pluralism in America.* New Brunswick, NJ: Transaction Publishers.

Rogers, C. R. (1980). *Becoming a person . . . Pt. 1. Some hypotheses regarding the facilitation of personal growth. Pt. 2. What it means to become a person.* (Originally published in 1956.) Austin, TX: Hogg Foundation for Mental Hygiene.

Rosedale, H., Langone, M., Bradshaw, R., & Eichel, S. (2015). The challenge of defining cult, *ICSA Today, 6*(3), 2–13).

Ross, J. (2010, August). *A legacy of shame: Luther and the Jews.* Retrieved from www.reformation21.org/articles/a-legacy-of-shame-luther-and-the-jews.php

Runciman, S. (2001). *A history of the Crusades.* London, UK: Folio Society.

Russell, B. (1957). *Why I am not a Christian and other essays on religion and related subjects.* London, UK: George Allen & Unwin.

Sagan, C. (1980) *Cosmos: Carl Sagan.* New York, NY: Ballantine Books.

Samples, K. R. (1994). *Prophets of the apocalypse: David Koresh and other American messiahs.* Grand Rapids, MI: Baker Books.

Scazzero, P. (2014). *Emotionally healthy spirituality: Unleash a revolution in your life in Christ.* Nashville, TN: Integrity.

Scazzero, P., & Bird, W. (2015). *The emotionally healthy church: A strategy for discipleship that actually changes lives.* Grand Rapids, MI: Zondervan.

Schaff, P. (1876/2014). *History of the Christian church.* New York, NY: Charles Scribner.

Schaeffer, F. A. (1968). *Escape from reason.* Downers Grove, IL. InterVarsity Press.

———. (1976). *How should we then live? The rise and decline of Western thought and culture.* Wheaton, IL: Crossway Books.

———. (2002) *Death in the city.* Wheaton, Ill: Crossway Books.

Shaw, D. (2014). *Traumatic narcissism relational systems of subjugation.* New York: Routledge, Taylor & Francis.

———. (2017c). Chapter 18: The relational system of the traumatizing narcissist. In L. Goldberg, W. Goldberg, R. Henry, & M. Langone, *Cult recovery: A clinician's guide to working with former members and families* (pp. 395–412). Bonita Springs, FL: ICSA.

Shelley, B. L. (1995). *Church history in plain language.* Dallas, TX: Word Publishing.

Sherman, J. (Writer); Wolochatiuk, T. (Dir.). (2006). *Jonestown: Paradise lost* (documentary, History Channel). New York, NY: A&E Home Video.

Simon, H. A. (1979). *Models of thought, vol. 1.* New Haven, CT: Yale University Press.

Singer, M. T. (1979, January). Coming out of the cults. *Psychology Today, 12,* 72–82.

———. (1990). Thought reform programs and the production of psychiatric casualties. *Psychiatric Annals, 20*(4), 188–93.

———. (1992). Undue influence and written documents: Psychological aspects. *Journal of Questioned Document Examination, 1*(1), 4–13.

———. (1993). In Langone, Preface, *Recovery from cults: Help for victims of psychological and spiritual abuse* (pp. xv–xix). New York, NY: W.W. Norton.

Singer, M. T. & Lalich, J. (1995). *Cults in our midst: The hidden menace in our everyday lives.* San Francisco, CA: Jossey-Bass.

Singer, M. T., Temerlin, M., & Langone, M. L. (1990). Psychotherapy cults. *Cultic Studies Journal, 7*(2), 101–25. Available online at https://drive.google.com/file/d/oB4dmoPK1tYNjQTJtc3EtVFpRdUo/edit

Sire, J. W. (2009*). The universe next door* (5th ed.). (Originally published in 1976.) Downers Grove, IL: International Varsity Press.

Sirkin, M. I. (1990). Cult involvement: A systems approach to assessment and treatment. *Psychotherapy: Theory, Research, Practice, Training, 27*(1), 116–23.

Slick, M. (n.d.). Pelagianism. Christian Apologetics & Research Ministry (CARM). Available online at https://carm.org/pelagianism

Speed, J. (2015). Burned over? Revivalism and its effects on the local church (Gospel Spam blog entry). Available online at http://gospelspam.com/burned-over-revivalism-and-its-effects-on-the-local-church/

Stark, R. (2014). *How the West was won: The neglected story of the triumph of modernity.* Wilmington, DE: ISI Books.

Stark, R., & Bainbridge, W. S. (1985). *The future of religion: Secularization, revival and cult formation.* Berkeley, CA: University of California Press.

Stark, R., & Corcoran, K. E. (2014). *Religious hostility: A global assessment of hatred and terror.* Waco, TX: ISR Books.

Stein, A. (2017). *Terror, love and brainwashing: Attachment in cults and totalitarian systems.* New York, NY: Routledge.

Stetzer, E. (2017, Feb. 25). The Exchange blog. What are these "five solas" and why do they even matter? An interview with college church pastor Josh Moody. Available online at https://www.christianitytoday.com/edstetzer/2017/february/centered-on-god.html

Tanner, J., & Tanner, S. (1989). *The changing world of Mormonism: A condensation and revision of Mormonism: Shadow or reality?* Chicago, IL: Moody Press.

Taylor, K. (2004). *Brainwashing: The science of thought control.* New York, NY: Oxford University Press.

Thibodeau, D., & Whiteson, L. (1999). *A place called Waco: A survivor's story.* New York, NY: Public Affairs.

Tobias, M. L., & Lalich, J. (1994). *Captive hearts, captive minds: Freedom and recovery from cults and abusive relationships.* Alameda, CA: Hunter House.

Tolkien, J. R. R. (1965). *The return of the king* [Part 3 of *Lord of the Rings* trilogy]. New York, NY: Ballantine Books.

VanVonderen, J. (2010). *Families where grace is in place: Building a home free of manipulation, legalism and shame.* Minneapolis, MN: Bethany House.

VanVonderen, J., Ryan, D., & Ryan J. (2008). *Soul repair: Rebuilding your spiritual life.* Downers Grove, IL: InterVarsity Press.

Veenhuizen, G. R. (2011). *Spiritual abuse: When the system becomes the persecutor.* (Doctoral dissertation, George Fox University, Newberg, OR). Retrieved from http://digitalcommons.georgefox.edu/cgi/viewcontent.cgi?article=1011&context=dmin

Viswanathan, Sandya (Dir.). (2009, August). Cults: dangerous devotion: Scholars and survivors discuss the mystery of cults. *Decoding the Past* television series (Season 3, Episode 2), History Channel.

Walsh, F. (2003). *Normal family processes growing diversity and complexity.* New York, NY: Guilford Press.

Watts, J. (2011). *Recovering from religious abuse.* New York, NY: Simon & Schuster.

References

Webster, D. D. (1999). *Soulcraft: How God shapes us through relationships.* Downers Grove, IL: InterVarsity Press.

Westminster Assembly of Divines. (1647/1976). *Westminster Confession of Faith.* (London; reprinted in 1976.) Glasgow, Scotland: Free Presbyterian.

Whitsett, D. P. (2017d). A modern psychodynamic approach with first-generation former cult members. In L. Goldberg, W. Goldberg, R. Henry, & M. Langone (Eds.), *Cult recovery: A clinician's guide to working with former members and families* (pp. 191–213). Bonita Springs, FL: ICSA.

Wickliff, M. (1989, December). Dysfunctional families: A framework for cult membership. In *The Shield* (Vol. 3, No. 4), pp. 1, 4, 5. Available online at http://www.dtl.org/cults/article/dysfunctional.htm

Wilkinson, M. (2010). *Changing minds in therapy: emotion, attachment, trauma, and neurobiology.* New York: Norton.

Winell, M. (1993). *Leaving the fold.* Berkeley, CA: Apocryphile.

Wright, K. (2001). *Religious abuse: A pastor explores the many ways religion can hurt as well as heal.* Kelowna, BC: Northstone.

Wright, R. K. M. (1996). *No place for sovereignty: What's wrong with freewill theism.* Downers Grove, IL: InterVarsity Press.

Yalom, I. D. (1985). *The theory and practice of group psychotherapy.* New York, NY: Basic Books.

Zablocki, B. D., & Robbins, T. (2001). *Misunderstanding cults: Searching for objectivity in a controversial field.* Toronto, Canada; Buffalo, NY: University of Toronto Press.

Ziegler, J. J. (2014). Pope: Ancient heresy plagues modern Church: Today's Pelagians are convinced that "salvation is the way I do things" [OurSundayVisitor blog, *OSV Newsweekly*]. Retrieved from https://www.osv.com/OSVNewsweekly/Story/TabId/2672/ArtMID/13567/ArticleID/14079/Pope-Ancient-heresy-plagues-modern-Church.aspx

Subject Index

Confession of Faith, of the Westminster
    Assembly of Divines, xxiii, 57
Constantine, 8
contextual approach, xxvii
controlling behaviors, devaluing the
    mind, 90
Conversionist conceptualization
    autobiographic support for, 74
    beliefs and ideas mattering, xxvi
    evaluating emotion affirmation, 77–78
    general revelation evaluation, 73–74
    literature review, 29–35
    on redemptive profit evaluation, 81
    of religious abuse, xxv–xxvi
    resting with choices of individuals, 67
    special revelation evaluation, 67–69
    strengths and limitations of, 115
    as a theoretical perspective, 21, 22
    weakest support for emotions in
        recovery, 79
Corcoran, Katie, 18, 19
core recovery needs, 98–109
correspondence view of truth, 128, 136
cosmos, as a cause-and-effect closed
    system, 54
countercult, defined, 136
countercult apologists, using theological
    arguments, 31
Counterfeit Revival (Hanegraaff), 34
Creator, dependence upon, 85
creed over deed, 31, 136
Crusades (1096–1291), 8–9
culpability, laid upon abusive groups or
    person(s), 29, 66
cult(s), 24–25, 136
cult apologists, 29, 136
Cult Education Institute website, 144
cult of confession, as a theme of mind
    control, 23
Cult Proofing Your Kids (Martin), 28
Cult Recovery: A Clinician's Guide
    (Goldberg, L., Goldberg, W.,
    Henry, R., & Langone, M.), 35,
    36–37
Cult Recovery: A Clinician's Guide
    (Henry), 132

*Cult Recovery: A Clinician's Guide to
    Working with Former Members
    and Families* (Shaw), 38
cult recruitment, models of, 37
cult sympathizers, 29, 136
cultic patterns, features of, 32–33
cultic studies, 24, 51, 128, 133, 144–46
*Cults in Our Midst: The Hidden Menace
    in Our Everyday Lives* (Singer &
    Lalich), 24
cultural influences upon the church,
    resources on, 149
cultural pluralism, expounded by Adam
    Smith, 19–20
current members of abusive groups, 110

daily needs, addressing, 99, 107–9, 111,
    112, 113
Darkness to Light (DTL) website, 145
deed over creed, 31, 136
deism, 13, 51, 53–54, 137
deliberative approach, 125
deliberative model, of cult recruitment, 37
deliberative or Conversionist
    conceptualization. *See*
    Conversionist conceptualization
demand for purity, as a theme of mind
    control, 23
Democratic Workers Party (DWP), 43
dentists, contributing health advice, 108
Denver Veterans Administration Medical
    Center, 94
destructive emotions, changing, 88
detrimental dependency, creating, xxiv
developmental growth, seven influential
    areas for, 127
dialogical (person centered) elements, 62
"Dispelling the Myths: The Psychological
    Consequences of Cultic
    Involvement" (Martin), 27–28
dispensing of existence, as a theme of
    mind control, 23
"divine authority," as a theme of mind
    control, 23
divine humanism, within a New Age
    worldview, 56
doctors, contributing health advice, 108

the "lost child," 97

love of God, use of our minds reflecting, 91

love-bombing, 30, 138

Luther, Martin, 11, 12, 105

The Making of a Moonie—Brainwashing of Choice? (Barker), 30

man, dependent on the Creator, xxiii

marital roles, relational resources redefining, 103

marriage, resources for the SECURE Approach, 147–48

marriage therapy, EFT as a successful form of, 132

Martin, Paul, 22, 25, 26, 27–29

Martin, Walter, 29, 31, 32, 33

the "mascot," 97

McLaren, Karla, 45

MeadowHaven, 41, 42, 74, 146

members, of an abusive religious group in Stage 1 of recovery, 110

mental, inappropriate boundary, 97

mental health professionals, providing specific guidelines, 36

mentoring, received by the author, 85

meta-narrative, 138

metaphysics, xxiii, 57

metaphysics/ontology, 138

Middle Ages (AD 590–517), 6, 8–10

Midrash, commentary on the Tanakh, 53

milieu control, as a theme of mind control, 23

mind, role of, 90

mind control

    basic behavioral definition, xxiv

    as a primary factor in spiritual abuse, 72

    Robert Lifton's concept of, xxiii–xxiv

    role of, xxiii, 49

    secular understanding of, 66

mind-control, victimization point of view, 21

mind-control adherents, xxvi

mind-control dynamics, Christians affirming, 67

mind-control perspective, 28

mind-control/thought-reform, xxv, 138

minds, using as a form of worship toward God, 91

Mishnah, summary of the laws of the Jews, 53

models, of cult recruitment, 37

modern-day Christianity, as moving toward hyped-up feelings, fantasy, and esoteric revelation, 34

monism, 52, 55

monotheism, 51, 52–53, 56, 57

moral relativism, in the Eastern notion of Karma, 56

morality, emotions as a crucial part of, 88

Mormons, 74

Mount Carmel Center, 16

Moyer, Bill, 24

mystical manipulation or "planned spontaneity," as a theme of mind control, 23

myths, 28

narcissistic leadership, false teleology originating from, 59

National Institute for the Psychotherapies (NIP), 37

natural evidence, 75, 76

naturalism, 51, 54

negative emotions, as energy draining, 107

negative-reinforcement feedback loop, 96

neutrality, lack of complete, 49

New Age worldview, 52, 56

New England Institute of Religious Research (NEIRR), Pardons as directors of, 40

New Religious Movements: A Practical Introduction (Barker), 30–31

new religious movements (NRMs), 30–31, 138

New Testament, examples of religious abuse, 4

Newton, John, 124

Nicene Creed, 56

Nietzsche, Friedrich, 54

nihilism, 52, 54–55

9/11, events of, 17

thought-reform/mind-control
  perspective
  general revelation evaluation, 72–73
  literature review, 22–29
  on redemptive profit evaluation, 80–81
  special revelation evaluation, 66–67
  strengths and limitations of, 114–15
time, as unreal in pantheistic monism, 55
a time to heal, mentioned in Ecclessiastes,
  95
timeline, creation of, 40
Tobias, Madeleine, 45
Tolkien, J. R. R., 125
totalist, aberrant Christian organization
  (TACO), religious abuse in, 85
totalitarian abuse, 16, 23
a transcendent belief system, construct
  of, 44
transference, xxv, 140
transformation, as an inside-out job, 5
trauma, relating to religious abuse and
  recovery, 39
trauma recovery
  resources for the SECURE Approach,
  152
  value of relational support for, 120
*Traumatic Narcissism: Relational Systems
  of Subjugation* (Shaw), 38
traumatizing narcissist, 38
*Treatise Concerning the Religious
  Affections* (Edwards), 13
triggers, 89, 106–7, 140
Trinitarian doctrine of God, 118
"true self," emergence of, 82
truth
  ability to discern from falsehood, 81
  correspondence view of assumed, 128
  false or distorted notions of, 60
  naturalists denying any ultimate, 54
  New Age beliefs denying
  propositional, 56
  revealed by God, 60
twentieth century, 6, 15–17
twenty-first century, 17–20
Twenty-First Century-9/11, 6
Twin Towers, World Trade Center,
  destruction of, 17

unconditional acceptance, 100, 104, 111.
  See also acceptance
unconditional positive regard
  from a consistent Christian
  perspective, 93
  defined, 140
  from humanistic psychology, xxvii, 86
  necessary for recovery from religious
  abuse, 92–93
  in person-centered approaches to
  therapy, 119–20
undue influence. *See* mind control
unhealthy, closed/self-sealed system of
  influence, breaking away from, 48
unhealthy relationships, letting go of, 102
unhealthy religious systems, devaluing
  individual personality, 100
unhealthy roles, recognition members
  receive from, 96
Unification Church (Moonies), 26, 30
United States, experience of diversity
  within, 20
"unlocking mind control," basic keys to,
  26–27
Pope Urban II, control of the Holy Land
  and, 8

value system, of needs of the leaders, 48
Van Vonderen, Jeff, 43, 45, 46–49
Veenhuizen, Gary R., 3
verifiable beliefs, 57
victimization, reframing, 99
viewpoints, value of, xxviii
visual triggers, experiencing, 89

Waco Massacre, as a starting place, 2
The War of the Jews (Josephus), 7
Watts, Jack, 46
weak religious groups, 20
Wellspring Retreat and Resource Center,
  27, 146
Westernized mind sciences, pantheistic
  monism present within, 55
Westminster Confession of Faith (1647),
  defined, 140
Whitsett, Doni, 37, 38–40
Wilberforce, William, 105

Name Index

Name Index

Kerr, M. E., 146
Kierkegaard, Soren, 55, 137
Kilduff, M., 15
Kimble, Melvin, xxii
King, M., 16
Kirkpatrick, L. A., xxvii, 86, 87, 144
Klein, W. W., 147
Knapp, Heidi I., 124, 131, 132, 145
Knapp, Patrick J., xxii, xxiv, xxv, 61, 67,
    68, 69, 76, 85, 96, 97, 120, 130,
    145, 150
Koehn, A. J., 86
Kolk, B. van der, 152
Kropveld, Michael, 145
Kurian, G. T., 11

Lalich, Janja, xxiv, xxv, 1, 13, 14, 16, 21,
    24, 25, 29, 43–45, 46, 48, 67, 70,
    71, 73, 76, 77, 78, 80, 82, 83, 89
Langone, Michael, xxi, xxiv, xxv, 21, 25, 27,
    29, 31, 35–37, 69, 72, 82, 145, 150
Laymon, B., 76
Layton, D., xxi, 2, 15
Lee, Chris, 146
Lee, W. Y., 146
Lewis, C. S., 124
Lewis, G. R., 151
Lienesch, R., 18
Lifton, Robert Jay, xxiii, 16, 21, 22–24, 25,
    27, 28, 29, 32, 66, 67, 68, 72, 73,
    80, 101
Lindsey, Luna, 1, 18, 21, 25, 66, 73
Lobdell, William, 18, 74

Maalouf, A., 9
Macaulay, R., xxiii, 59, 151
MacCulloch, D., 11
Martin, Paul, xxv, 22, 25, 26, 27–29, 66,
    67, 80, 146
Martin, Stephen, 27
Martin, Walter, 6, 11, 16, 21, 29, 31,
    32–33, 34, 67, 68, 73, 78, 81
Matthews, B. L., 86
McFarlene, A., 152
McLaren, Karla, 43, 44, 45, 71, 76, 83
Meister, C. V., 143
Melton, J. G., 16, 21
Metaxas, E., 150

Miner, M. H., 87
Minuchin, S., 146
Moyer, Bill, 24
Murray, 15

Nee, W., 128
Newport, J. P., 61, 143
Newport, K., 16
Newton, John, 124, 149
Nichols, M. P., 146
Nietzsche, Friedrich, 54
Noll, Mark, 14

Ofshe, R., 73
Olsson, Peter A., 24
Orlowski, B. M., 17

Pardon, Judy, 40–42, 69, 70, 71, 74, 75,
    82, 146
Pardon, Robert (Bob), 40–42, 69, 70, 71,
    74, 75, 82, 146
Passantino, B., xxv, 69, 73
Passantino, G., xxv, 69, 73
Pement, Eric, 145
Pierce, R. W., 148
Pile, Lawrence, 27
Pine, R. C., 144
Pocwe, K. O., 17
Powers, H., 148
Psychology Harrassment Information
    Association, 24

Ramsay, P., 13
Regina, W. F., 76
Reisz, S., 119
Rhodes, R., xxv, 11
Rische, Jill Martin, 32
Rische, Kevin, 32
Robbins, T., 19, 73
Rogers, C. R., xxvii
Rogers, Carl, 86, 92
Rosedale, Herbert, xxi, 1, 25
Ross, J., 12
Ross, Rick A., 144, 152
Rothschild, J., 9
Runciman, S., 9
Russell, B., 54
Ryan, D., 149

Name Index

Ryan, Dale, 45
Ryan, J., 149
Ryan, Juanita, 45
Ryan, Patrick, 152

Sagan, Carl, 54
Sammons, Gregory, 146
Samples, K. R., 15, 16
Sanderfer, Kenneth, 132, 148
Sartre, Jean-Paul, 55, 137
Scazzero, P., 21
Schaeffer, F. A., 2, 7, 119, 148, 151
Schwartz, J. G., 147
Schwartz, R. C., 146
Shaff, Philip, 10
Shaw, Daniel, 21, 37–38, 69, 78, 82
Shelley, B. L., 8, 11, 12
Sherman, J., 15
Shupe, A. D., 73
Siegelman, J., 19
Siener-Ciesla, S., 86
Silver, N., 147
Simon, Herbert A., 44
Singer, Margaret Thaler, xxiv, xxv, 1, 13,
    14, 16, 21, 22, 24–25, 27, 29, 32,
    36, 43, 44, 67, 72, 73, 77, 80, 89
Sire, J., 144, 147
Sire, J. W., xxii, xxiii, 51, 53
Sirkin, M. I., 116
Slick, M., 15
Smith, Adam, 19–20
Smith, J. D., 11
Smith, J. E., 13
Stanton, M., 147
Stark, Rodney, 1, 2, 12, 17, 18, 19–20
Stein, A., 78
Stetzer, E., 11
Stewart, R. B., 143

TACO (Totalist Aberrant Christian
    Organization), 85
Tada, Joni Erickson, 149
Tanner, J., 1, 74
Tanner, S., 1, 74
Taylor, K., 21
Taylor, Kathleen, 25, 66, 77

Temerlin, Maurice, 25
Thibodeau, D., 2, 16, 18, 73
Thomas, G., 148
Tillapaugh, F. R., 148
Tobias, Madeleine Landau, 43, 44–45, 89
Tolkien, J. R. R., 125
Townsend, J. S., 103
TROP The Religion of Peace.com, 17

Vaillot, 15
VanVonderen, Jeff, xxiii, xxv, 3, 5, 21, 43,
    45, 46–49, 70, 71, 76, 79, 82, 83,
    94, 142, 147, 149
Veenhuizen, Gary R., 3, 76
Viswanathan, S., 24
Vujicic, Nick, 149

Walsh, F., xxviii, 146
Watts, Jack, 46, 94
Webster, D. D., 149
Weisaeth, L., 152
Wessinger, 16
Whiston, W., 7
Whiteson, L., 2, 16, 18, 73
Whitsett, Doni, 37, 38–40, 69, 82
Wickliff, M., 76, 116
Wilkinson,, 39
Williams, C. T., 86
Winell, M., 74
Wittmer, 16
Wolochatiuk, T., 15
Wright, K., 2
Wright, P., 1
Wright, R. K. M., 15, 69, 115, 123, 143,
    151

Yalom, I. D., xxv
Yerkovich, K., 148
Yerkovich, M., 148

Zablocki, B. D., 73
Zacharias, R. K., 6, 11
Zacharias, Ravi, 32
Zeolla, Gary, 145
Ziegler, J. J., 15

Index of Ancient Documents

Psalms *(cont.)*

69:29	88
86	63
95	88
115:3	125
119:105	118
138	88
139:13–16	104
145	88
145:8	121
145:14–17	59
147	88

Proverbs

2:1–5	118

Ecclesiastes

3:1–5	95

Isaiah

26:3	59, 91
49:15	93
55:8–11	61
61:8	118

Jeremiah

5:26–31	3
31:34	60
32:40–41	59

Lamentations

3:31–33	59

Ezekiel

34:1–6 NIV	4
34:1–24	3

Zechariah

11	3

ANCIENT JEWISH WRITERS

Josephus

The Antiquities of the Jews

30–650	7

Flavius Josephus Against Apion

926–73	7

The War of the Jews

651–925	7

NEW TESTAMENT

Matthew

3:16–17	118
4:4	118
4:10	60
5:-12	46
7:13	60
9:35–38	4
15:1–20	59
19:19	60
22:37–40	59, 60
23	122
24:20	60
26:36–38	121
27:45–50	121
28:19	118

Mark

6:33–34	4
12:30	91

Luke

10:21	121
11:42	59
15:1–2	4
15:1–7	150
15:11–32	150
16:15	59

Index of Ancient Documents

CPSIA information can be obtained
at www.ICGtesting.com
Printed in the USA
LVHW080027210622
721742LV00014B/820

9 781725 286498